Austrian Poetry Today

Österreichische Lyrik heute

For Jean,
who made it
clean.
Milne W5t

For Jean,
I haven't forgotten
your help and
kindness.
Harry

Austrian Poetry Today

Österreichische Lyrik heute

EDITED & TRANSLATED BY

Milne Holton & Herbert Kuhner

SCHOCKEN BOOKS

NEW YORK

In memory of

Mary Milne Holton (1900–1975)

Gisela Kuhner (1892–1979)

First published by Schocken Books 1985
10 9 8 7 6 5 4 3 2 1   85 86 87 88
Copyright © 1985 by Milne Holton and Herbert Kuhner

Library of Congress Cataloging in Publication Data
Main entry under title:
Austrian poetry today.
English and German.
Includes bibliographical references and index.
1. German poetry—Austrian authors—Translations into
English.   2. Austrian poetry (German)—Translations into
English.   3. German poetry—20th century—Translations
into English.   4. English poetry—Translations from
German.   5. German poetry—Austrian authors.   6. Austrian
poetry (German). 7. German poetry—20th century.
I. Holton, Milne. II. Kuhner, Herbert.
PT3824.Z5A8 1985   831'.914'08   83–20221

Designed by Cynthia Krupat
Manufactured in the United States of America
ISBN 0–8052–3903–0

CONTENTS

The New Generation

PREFACE

This collection was conceived several years ago when its editors met in Yugoslavia at the Struga Poetry Festival. There we first became aware of a mutually recognized need for the acknowledgment by anthology of the separable and vital tradition of contemporary Austrian poetry. We have since consulted with friends and associates too numerous to mention here, but of the many there are a few who deserve special thanks.

We would first acknowledge a special debt to the late Duško Tomovski, who encouraged us at the outset in Struga. Tomovski was a distinguished Macedonian translator and scholar who knew contemporary Austrian literature well; his passing was a loss to many, both in Austria and in his own country.

Dr. Heinz Lunzer and his capable staff at the Dokumentationstelle für neuere österreichische Literatur provided invaluable assistance in our background research. The Library of Congress, in Washington, D.C., made its excellent collection of German-language literatures available to us, and its Reader and Stack Division provided study facilities for the completion of the project.

Heinz Tomek of Austria Presse Agentur read the German texts and has been of great assistance in locating errors of transmission and in textual selection. Prof. George Steiner of Cambridge University and Dr. Jean Nordhaus of Washington, D.C., read the entire manuscript and made their invaluable comments available to us. Thanks are also due to Profs. William MacBain and John Fuegi of the University of Maryland, to Dr. Max Demeter Peyfuss of the Institut für Ost- und Südwesteuropaforschung of the University of Vienna, and to Frau Irene Voigt and Wolfgang Herles of Vienna, all of whom gave us the benefit of their useful suggestions. Thorburn Reid III of Washington, D.C., was of vital assistance in last-minute research. Of course, errors are the sole responsibility of the editors.

We would also like to express our gratitude to Dr. Hans J. Marte; to Dr. Peter Marginter; and to Frau Helga Schmid of the Cultural-Political Section of the Austrian Federal Ministry for Foreign Affairs; to Dr. Hermann Mayer, director of the Literary Section of the Austrian Ministry of Education and Art; to Dr. Fritz Cocron, director of the Austrian Institute in New York; to Dr. Bernhard Stillfried, director of the Austrian Institute in London; to Dr. Valentin Inzko, Austrian cultural attaché in Belgrade; and to Dr. Heinrich Haymerle, former Austrian ambassador to the United Nations, for their help and encouragement. We also wish to express our sincere gratitude to the Austrian Federal Ministry for Foreign Affairs, the Austrian Ministry of Education and Art, the Creditanstalt-Bankverein, the Österreichische Länderbank AG, and Mr. Peter Rath of Lobmeyr, Vienna, for their generous support of this publication.

Frau Gerda Maleter of Vienna and Frau Maria Pink of *Kleine Zeitung*, Klagenfurt, assisted us in obtaining translation rights. Ruth Doerflein of Washington, D.C., and the secretarial staff of the English Department of the University of Maryland capably prepared the manuscript. Sylvia Holton has tolerated our disputatious work sessions, both in Washington and in Vienna, with equanimity.

Thanks are also due to the poets and publishers who have cooperated in our enterprise; their names are listed in the Acknowledgments.

WMH & HK

INTRODUCTION

In an introductory essay to a remarkable survey of postwar Austrian writing, Hans Wolfschütz has taken as the beginning of his period of concern the year 1943. Wolfschütz reports that Dr. Adolf Schärf (who would later become Austria's third postwar president) identified that year as the time during which he realized that Austria was no longer part of a greater Germany, indeed that the idea of a Republic of Austria as an autonomous and permanently separate European state was a viable concept.[1] That such an awareness should come so late to a man such as Schärf is on its face astounding, but it is less so if one remembers how generally unsatisfactory was the conception of what had been originally designated as "Deutsch Österreich" (and later came to be known as the First Republic), almost an afterthought following the dismemberment of Imperial Austria in 1918. For it seemed destined from the very beginning that the First Republic, after enduring twenty years of bitter party conflict, would acquiesce, exhausted, in its own demise in the election preceding the *Anschluß* of 1938.

The Austria of the Second Republic, the Austria established by a new constitution in 1945, was a country much more circumspect in the preservation of its democratic integrity. Ruled by a coalition government until 1966, her policy remained undisturbed by extremists from left or right—with the exception of the Communist strikes of 1950, after which a more moderate socialism prevailed. Membership in the Organization for European Cooperation and Development (OECD) came in 1953; in 1955 the Austrian State Treaty, which guaranteed Austria's neutrality, was signed by the great powers of East and West in the thaw that followed Stalin's death. And since the impetus of the Marshall Plan in the immediate postwar years, Austria has enjoyed a steadily developing prosperity.

Yet as late as 1963 questions were still being raised about the autonomy of her literature. When a conservative critic like Herbert Eisenreich asked in that year, "Ist Österreichs Literatur eine österreichische Literatur?" he restated a concern that was being expressed with increasing frequency in the decades after World War II.[2] Before those years—indeed, even in the high years of the Habsburg Empire—it was never really established as a certainty that Austrian literature was a separately viable tradition. Somehow, however, in those prosperous and circumspect years of the Second Republic, that autonomous Austrian literature has become an irrefutable certainty.

1. Hans Wolfschütz and Alan Best, eds., *Modern Austrian Writing* (London and Totowa, N.J., 1980), pp. 1–20. Wolfschütz's essay, and the others collected here, are of great use to the student of Austrian writing in the postwar period.
2. "Das schöpferische Mißtrauen oder Ist Österreichs Literatur eine österreichische Literatur?," an essay in his *Reaktionen* (Gütersloh, 1964), pp. 72–105.

Of course there have existed for several centuries the cultural, historical, religious, and even linguistic conditions from which an autonomous literature could be expected. Although in the post–World War II years it had become a continually receding subject, the long history of the Habsburgs lay in Austria's past. Ivar Ivask has mentioned the very presence of Vienna as a cultural and political center as a distinguishing characteristic of Austrian culture in the German-speaking world.[3] And of course there is Austria's now somewhat diminished ethnic and linguistic diversity, a diversity which has assured for her artistic and intellectual communities a linguistic self-consciousness which has generated both Wittgensteinian speculation and dialectical experiment in plays, novels, and poems. Even the Catholicism of the Austrians continues today to be a shaping literary influence in some quarters.

There are other qualities that are less facilely explained: the importance of the novel, of comedy, and of theater to the Austrian writers, the absence of literary naturalism, the special delight in "black humor," the curious concern with the isolated self.[4] The features have been apparent since the war in the quite clearly identifiable Austrian fiction and in the remarkably vital, although somewhat less distinct Austrian drama. Yet the distinctiveness and vitality of contemporary Austrian poetry has yet to be established, especially for the American and English reader.

The distinctiveness of contemporary Austrian poetry—and it is to our minds no less distinct than Austrian drama or fiction—is firmly rooted in the past. Quite clearly there is a viably Austrian modernist tradition, traceable at least as far back as the beginning of this century. This modernist tradition had its masters: Rilke and Hofmannsthal and Trakl, though their impact was felt well beyond her borders, were all distinctively Austrian. Rilke, the cosmopolitan of Imperial Prague, had a long and developing career which manifested many influences. Hofmannsthal, manifestly the Viennese bourgeois intellectual, wrote symbolist verse mainly at the beginning of his career, the last decade of the nineteenth century. Georg Trakl was dead in 1914 after a poetic career of only seven years, but the dark imagination of this *poète maudit* of Salzburg, his reading of Rimbaud, and his resultant decadent expressionism left an indelible mark on the Austrian poetic imagination.

In the next generation there were even more expressionistically committed poets—poets like Franz Werfel, whom Rilke had praised, or Theodor Däubler, born in Austro-Hungarian Trieste and always vaguely Italianate. In the 1920s and 1930s some Austrian poets turned toward more traditional, even more pastoral, concerns, poets like Anton Wildgans or Josef Weinheber (who was somewhat discredited after World War II); their opposition to the urban and expressionist painter-poets of Vienna, like Albert

3. Ivar Ivask, "Austrian Literature," in *Encyclopedia of World Literature in the Twentieth Century,* edited by Wolfgang Bernard Fleischmann (3 vols.; New York, 1967–1971), 1: 70–82, 71. This essay has been germinal in defining the directions of Austrian literature to English readers.
4. Ivask has noted all these characteristics. See ibid., pp. 71–72.

Paris Gütersloh, reflected the deep intellectual and political divisions of the First Austrian Republic. Perhaps it was Karl Kraus, the political satirist and epigrammatist, and editor of the one-man magazine *Die Fackel,* who most trenchantly embodied and recorded the tensions of these decades.

The pastoral poets and the classicists are not frequently spoken of today. Weinheber, who in 1934 was hailed as the successor to Hofmannsthal and Rilke, is no longer widely read, although one of course wonders to what extent Weinheber is to be taken as one source for the recent vogue for poetry in the Viennese dialect.[5] Ernst Waldinger and Theodor Kramer, who both emigrated during the Nazi years, remain neglected by Austrian critics. It is probably no surprise that after the war the resurgence of interest in expressionism, surrealism, and dada—traditions long ignored in Austria, then proscribed by the Nazis—seems now a bit exclusivist. But the Austrian delight in satire has continued undiminished.[6]

Yet poetry in postwar Austria was not simply a reaction to or a recovery of its own past after a decade of silence or exile. Among the poets after the war there was an almost immediate response to their present, to the Austria of the Second Republic, which was emerging as a modern, post-ideological, consumer society. The poets saw Vienna—emptied of her Jewish intellectuals and many of her young people, her press devitalized and many of her writers abroad where they had found larger audiences and better pay—as a capital of little more than a certain retrospective propriety; Vienna's great strength, her spirit of restless inquiry and experiment, seemed to have gone with the winds of war. For the writers and poets who remained the situation seemed to call for desperate measures.[7]

Their response was a flamboyant, even perhaps a desperately dadaist one. In the early 1950s a number of young Viennese poets—H. C. Artmann, Ernst Jandl, Friederike Mayröcker, and others—formed a circle around Andreas Okopenko and his *publikationen,* a journal in which a number of them were published; by 1952, out of this circle, a group of friends—Gerhard Rühm, Artmann, Oswald Wiener, Konrad Bayer, and somewhat later, Friedrich Achleitner—formed a collaboration to be known as the "Wiener Gruppe," or "Vienna Group." In part they proceeded on the basis of an expressionist/surrealist aesthetic set forth for painters by Gütersloh and the so-called School of Fantastic Realists and promulgated by his "art club."[8] But the Vienna Group—whose avant-garde advocacy of radical linguistic procedures, anarchist politics, and post-Brechtian dramaturgy was apparent first in their rather grotesque bohemianism, later in manifestations

5. See Harald Gröhler, "Letter from Germany," *Dimension* 4, no. 1 (1974): 8–7, 12.
6. In this summary we owe much to Ivask, "Austrian Literature."
7. Perhaps the most thoughtful recent study of the modern Austrian experience is Felix Kreissler's *La prise de conscience de la nation autrichienne,* 2 vols. (Paris, 1980). The second volume is concerned with the post–World War II period.
8. Frederick Ungar's *Handbook of Austrian Literature* (New York, 1971), pp. 105–7 contains a splendid short essay on Gütersloh by the distinguished Austrian writer and critic Herbert Eisenreich (who has also been cited above). Ungar's collection is a valuable tool in the study of modern Austrian literature by English readers.

which anticipated the "happenings" of the 1960s—were really never theoretically unified. They began to disperse around 1960: Rühm became committed to *Konkretismus* and left Vienna; Artmann turned toward dialect poetry, became fascinated with language, and lived in various places throughout Europe after 1960. Upon the death of Konrad Bayer, who committed suicide in 1964, the Vienna Group ceased its activities. But the members remained friends and continued their diverse individual work, and Jandl and Mayröcker stayed in Vienna.[9]

Of course many of Austria's finest poets had been living abroad for some time, long before the Vienna Group had been thought of. Paul Celan was in Paris, becoming increasingly aware of the totality of European culture (he was a disciple of Rilke in this respect if in no other); Erich Fried remained in London and worked there after the war.[10] Others, some still in Austria, stood apart from any group—Thomas Bernhard, a notorious "loner,"[11] and Ingeborg Bachmann, whose existential and philosophical awarenesses made her Rilke's most probable successor. And there were conservatives and traditionalists, poets like Ernst Schönwiese and the distinguished and rather metaphysical women poets Christine Lavant and Christine Busta. Jutta Schutting, whose poems are reflective in style and subject, would have her first collection introduced by Schönwiese as late as 1973.[12] So in the decades which followed the war the Austrian poets, although various and diverse, were vital and awake.

In the early 1960s the prosperity of postwar Austria seemed still beset by doubts. Many social problems, among them inadequate housing and the need for educational reform, remained unsolved. There were inefficiencies in state-owned industries, even as the economy boomed. Young Austrians, those who had grown up since the war, were restless and aware of the activities of their counterparts in other countries. Poets were among the first to give voice to these discontents. Around 1960 a new movement began in Austrian poetry, its place of origin distinctly not Vienna. This movement was to generate a "resonance" in Austrian poetry which, as Harald Gröhler put it in 1974, "extends at the present time over all German speaking lands."[13]

The movement was formed at first around the improbable figure of Alfred Kolleritsch, then a thirty-year-old teacher in Graz who conducted a course in literature in the Municipal College in that city. In 1960 Kolleritsch began to edit and to publish *manuskripte,* and he attracted to the pages of his journal a number of talented Graz writers, among them Peter Handke, who

9. See Gröhler, "Letter from Germany," and Peter Demetz, *Postwar German Literature: A Critical Introduction* (New York, 1972), pp. 24–32.
10. Essays on Celan and Fried (by Wolfschütz and Rex Last, respectively) appear in Wolfschütz and Best, eds., *Modern Austrian Writing.*
11. Wolfschütz also has an essay on Bernhard in *Modern Austrian Writing.*
12. For a discussion of these poets in a recent review, see Rex Last, "Tradition and Experiment," *TLS,* June 11, 1976, p. 716.
13. Gröhler, "Letter from Germany," p. 8.

was then studying law in Graz. When the group managed an exhibition in an arts center in the town, they came to be known as "Forum Stadtpark" and their circle grew. Their antibourgeois politics and their appetite for dramatic, prosodic, and linguistic experiment attracted a number of Vienna Group poets; the Graz Group grew beyond Graz, and soon H. C. Artmann was an important and influential figure among them. Handke's *Publikumsbeschimpfung* [Offending the audience] (1966) first appeared in *manuskripte,* as did Oswald Wiener's *Die Verbesserung vom Mitteleuropa* [The improvement of Central Europe]; the dramatist Wolfgang Bauer was first published in *manuskripte,* and many experiments in "Konkretismus" appeared in its pages.[14]

Handke later moved in the direction of more conventional literary techniques and beyond the Graz Group, and he has now found a wide international audience. But in the early 1970s other Graz Group writers—many of whom were no longer in Graz—gained a wider audience when a number of West German publishers, notably Suhrkamp and Rowohlt, began to publish their work. These German houses were followed by Residenz Verlag in Salzburg. By 1973 the Graz experimentalists were strong enough to form an organization, first known as the "Graz Authors' Congress" (and identified by the Austrian press as the "Austrian Anti-P.E.N. Club"), later renamed the "Graz Authors' Collective." The Collective gained a sizable membership, including Artmann, Rühm, Jandl, and Mayröcker, as well as, of course, Kolleritsch. Jandl called the Austrian P.E.N. Club "a disgrace for the International P.E.N. Club and for Austria." The traditionalists used Reinhard Federmann's magazine, rather rudely named *Die Pestsäule* [The plague column], for their reply. Today the experimentalist Graz Group writers have access to the West German publishers and specific houses in Austria while the traditionalists remain in control of Austrian P.E.N., whose membership may now be no larger than that of the Collective. Although the combatants have given some recent evidence of wearying with the struggle, the air is still heavy where poetry is being written today in Austria.

It is not our purpose here to join in the disputes of Austrian literary politics, and it is therefore certainly not to be our undertaking to separate further the already-divided Austrian poets. Rather we shall follow the Viennese psychiatrists in assuming the formative nature of experience and in therefore dividing our poets into "generations" which bring together those poets who have shared historical experiences in their early years. We believe that it is this shared experience in history, not literary or political allegiance, which should form the reader's basis for comparison. Through this arrangement we hope to communicate an awareness of the development—not only to dramatize the struggles—of Austrian poetry in the past two decades.

14. For a full statement of the Graz Group's concerns, see Peter Laemmle and Jorg Drews, *Wie die Grazer auszogen, die Literatur zu erobern* (München, 1975). Also see Hugh Rorrison's essay in Wolfschütz and Best, eds., *Modern Austrian Writing.*

We have accordingly identified four "generations" among the contemporary Austrian poets: "The Older Generation" (those born before 1912), "The Generation of the War" (those born in the years between 1912 and 1923), "The Postwar Generation" (most of whom were born between 1924 and 1938, the year of the *Anschluß),* and "The New Generation" (most of these poets were born after 1938). In our grouping of poets for presentation here we have been only more or less faithful to our chronological parameters. Our real purpose has been to bring together into groups those poets old enough to remember Imperial Austria, those whose central experience is that of World War II, those who are young enough to have escaped that formative trauma and yet who know enough of it to think of themselves as living in the "postwar" period, and those who seem not to have any formative experience which is the direct result of the war or its aftermath. Since we have defined ours as a collection of "contemporary" poets, we have, with one exception,[15] excluded from consideration any poet who died before 1964, the year of Konrad Bayer's suicide. We have also excluded those postwar writers known principally as novelists, who only on occasion wrote poetry—novelists like Alexander Lernet-Holenia and Heimito von Doderer. We have included some poets simply because we admire their work, even though we recognized that they had not—or have not yet—commanded a sufficient readership or established sufficient "importance" so that they could be fairly identified as "major" or even as "representative" Austrian poets. So our selection of poets is just that—a selection; it is not to be regarded as representative in any defining or restricting way. The decades of Austrian poetry which we confront here are simply too rich and too diverse.

Our undertaking has been to present poems not before translated into English whenever possible. Thus we have avoided presenting once again poems such as Paul Celan's "Todesfuge" or Ingeborg Bachmann's "Grosse Landschaft bei Wien." These poems, and there are certainly others like them, are of importance not only to Austrian poetry but to poetry in many languages; they have been well translated into English more than once, and there is no reason to offer yet another translation here. What is to our minds of more importance is the presentation of new poems, poems of which English and American readers may well have been aware but which were hitherto unavailable in translation. The contemporary poetry of the Austrians (a people fewer in number than the Bavarians, as has been too frequently observed) has had a striking impact on other poetry being written in German today. Earlier Austrian poets—in translation—have shaped poetic developments in both France and in the English-speaking world. It is not surprising that like their predecessors—like Rilke and Trakl and Hofmannsthal—the contemporary Austrian poets have considerable impact in the world beyond their country's narrow borders.

15. The exception is Hertha Kräftner, Austria's Sylvia Plath, who committed suicide in 1951 and was almost forgotten until 1977, when Andreas Okopenko's and Otto Breicha's collection of her work was republished. Only then did her poems find a wide readership.

The Older Generation

Vorwort

Manchmal neben dem Hammer
liegt eine Feder.
Da wird die Faust zu Hand,
zu Papier die Wand,
und in die Hofkammer
blicken Cypresse und Zeder.

"ALBERT PARIS GÜTERSLOH"

(1887–1973)

One of the fascinating artistic and literary figures in Vienna of the twentieth century, and one of the earliest of the expressionists in European literature, was Albert Conrad Kiehtrieber or, "Albert Paris Gütersloh." Gütersloh studied painting with Gustav Klimt, collaborated with Max Reinhardt as a stage designer, and worked in Vienna during World War I at press headquarters on Robert Musil's recommendation. After the First World War Gütersloh lived and painted for a time in the south of France, then in 1929 became a professor at the School of Industrial Arts in Vienna.

Gütersloh's literary career, like his painting, was expressionistically oriented. His *Die tanzende Törin* [The dancing fool] (1910) was one of the founding works of Austrian literary expressionism, and his essay on Egon Schiele (1911) was a shaping document in Austrian art history. After World War I Gütersloh published a periodical, *Die Rettung* [The rescue], and he was awarded the Fontane Prize for his important novel *Der Lügner unter Bürgern* [The liar beneath the citizen] of 1923.

But then he fell silent, or at least for a time wrote only reviews and essays for various journals. It was primarily because of his painting that, after the *Anschluß,* he was identified by the Nazis as a "degenerate artist" and was silenced, isolated, and made to work first as a laborer, then as a clerk during the Second World War.

After that war he was appointed professor, later rector, of the Academy of Fine Arts in Vienna. In 1946 he published a complex and difficult novel and in 1947 a collection of short stories. A friend of the novelist and aesthetician Heimito von Doderer, Gütersloh was also in 1946 the president of the "art club" which would later help shape the Vienna Group. In 1961 he published another collection of stories, *Laßt uns den Menschen machen* [Let us make man], and in 1962 he reestablished himself as a major presence in Austrian letters with *Sonne und Mond* [Sun and moon], his great "historical novel of the present" and his aesthetic *summa. Der Lügner unter Bürgern* was translated as *The Fraud* in 1965. He wrote another novel, *Kain und Abel* (1969) and a crucial document in recent criticism, *Malerei des phantastischen Realismus* [Painters of fantastic realism] (1964). Gütersloh died in 1973. His later poems—and he had written poetry throughout his career—were published in 1975 in *Treppe ohne Haus: oder Seele ohne Leib* [Staircase without a house: or a soul without a body].

Preface

Sometimes next to a hammer,
a pen.
Fist becomes hand,
wall turns to paper
and from your courtyard room
glimpses of cypress and cedar.

Da wirst du Armer
zum Allerbarmer,
gibst Jedem das Seine,
dazu noch das Deine,
und was dir bleibt ist das Nichts
des Gedichts.

Der Jüngling erwacht

Als der Niederfall
immer neuer Gesetzestafeln
nicht aufhörte zu fallen,
und das dazwischenfallende Licht
die Menschheit wie Sträflinge scheckte
da erhob sich mein Ich,
und schrieb auf eine lange Säule
seine Eigentumlichkeit.

August des Lebens

Wenn die Zeit reif ist,
öffnet sich
nichts als ein Mund,
und die Frucht fällt
wie ein Knebel heraus.

Intuition

Innwärts rollender Bergsturz
grollend lang.
Wie Meilerrauch rieselt
verschüttete Seele
tausendspaltig herauf.

Als Alexandra vierzehn Jahre wurde

Heute läutet dir
eine Glocke
in der höchsten Spitze des Weltraums.

Then you who are poor
become the poorest of the poor;
you give to each his own
and give your own as well,
which leaves you with the Nothing
that is poetry.

The Boy Awakens

With the continuous crumbling
of ever new commandments
and with light
falling between,
mottling mankind
like prisoners,
my Being stood up
and carved on a high column
its Selfhood.

August of Life

When the time is ripe
nothing but a mouth
opens
and the fruit falls out
like a gag.

Intuition

An incessantly rumbling avalanche
rolls toward the River Inn.
The buried soul
rises upward
through thousands of crevices
like smoke.

Alexandra's Fourteenth Birthday

Today a bell
rings for you
in the highest place

Dann fällt sie wie eine Blume vom Stengel
hinaus in die Nacht.

Aus deinem Schicksal gegossen,
auf deinen Namen gestimmt,
für diesen Tag in den Mittag gehängt
zwischen zwei Ewigkeiten,
erschüttert sie dich allein.

Ferne von Dir
falte ich meine Hände
wie zerbröckelndes Gemäuer
in der Tiefe zusammenkommt.

in the universe
and falls like a flower
from its stem
out into the night.

Cast out of your fate
tuned to your name;
hung in the noon of this day,
between two eternities,
it shatters you alone.

Far from you
I clasp my hands,
as crumbling walls
come together in their depths.

Haute Couture des Gedichts

Wenn er winkt mit dem Finger,
der Dior der Poesie,
schrumpft zu Shorts,
zu Bikinis die Dichtung.
Oder sie dehnt sich
zur Fülle des Ballkleids,
des bodenlangen,
stürzen am Markte
die Kurse der
Mini-Poeme.
O die neuen Gewänder des Kaisers,
gezaubert aus Wortzwischenräumen,
oder die letzten
Dessins des Gedichts,
gestückt aus
Fetzen der Silben!
Siehe, gefügig
den Launen des Handelsgotts,
regen die Scheren
die Zuschneider
und Midinetten
des Worts.

Der Christus von Kasan

Der Christus,
wie eine alte
Kasaner Handschrift ihn schildert,

WILHELM SZABO

(1901–)

Born in Vienna, Wilhelm Szabo worked until 1939 as a schoolmaster in Lower Austria. He wrote during the German occupation, but in 1945 he resumed teaching and has held various teaching and administrative posts in education in Weitra in Lower Austria since. Szabo is essentially a rural lyricist whose poems set forth the life of his region.

Szabo's first collection of poems appeared in 1933; his most recent, *Schallgrenze* [Sound barrier], appeared in 1974. Szabo is a member of the Austrian P.E.N. Club.

Haute Couture of Poetry

He need but crook his finger,
the Dior of poetry,
and in a jiffy
up go the skirts to mini height.
Or if it be his whim
down they plunge to maxi length,
and lo and behold,
mini poems drop to new lows
on the poetry market.
O the emperor's new clothes!
What'll it be this season?
Words laced with spaces
or frilled with punctuation
or pieced from rags of syllables?
With ears cocked
and scissors poised
the tailors wait at their tables
for the God of Commerce
to give them the word
so they can cut their cloth.

Christ of Kazan

Christ,
according to
an ancient Kazan script,

ist klein,
bucklig
und dunkelhäutig,
ein kümmerlicher,
langnäsiger Mann
mit schütterem
Haar und Bart
und schreckhaft zusammengewachsenen
dichten Brauen.

Sagte er uns,
wer er sei,
und zeigte als Ausweis die Wunden,
wir glaubten ihm nicht,
wir sprächen das Wort nicht
des Thomas:
Mein Herr und mein Gott!

Der Küster veranschlagt

Der Küster veranschlagt,
der Totengräber und Friedhofsbesorger
die restliche
Frist meines Lebens.
Der Sargtischler
rechnet mit mir und
einkalkuliert mich
der Kränze-, der
Grabsteinerzeuger.
Die schwarzgeränderten
Zettel des Druckers
warten auf
meinen Namen.

Du buchtest, Freund

Du buchtest, Freund,
einen Sitz für den Flug
nach Kanton, Tanking und Nanking,
erpicht darauf,
deine Schnappschüssesammlung
durch Aufnahmen von Pagoden,
Dschunken und Reisfeldern
zu bereichern.

is short,
hunchbacked,
and dark-skinned,
a wretched,
long-nosed man
with thinning
hair and beard,
closely knit brows,
and timid eyes.

Were he to tell us
who he is
and show his wounds as proof,
we'd not believe him
nor speak the words
of Thomas:
My Lord and my God!

The Sexton's Assessment

The sexton calculates
the time left for me,
just as the gravedigger
and the curator of the cemetery.
The coffin-maker waits for me
and figures out his estimate,
just as the florist
and the stonemason total up theirs.
the black-edged sheets
at the printer's
are waiting
for my name.

You, My Friend, Reserve

You, my friend, reserve
a seat on the flight
to Canton, Tanking, and Nanking,
eager to enrich
your snapshot collection
with photos of pagodas,
junks, and rice fields.

Ich doch,
der Ungereiste,
tröste mich mit dem Wort
eines Weisen jener Lande:
Ohne vors Tor
deines Hauses zu treten,
erkennst du die Welt.

But I,
a stay-at-home,
console myself with the words
of a wise man on those lands:
Without crossing
the threshold of your own house,
you apprehend the world.

———

Alles ist nur ein Bild
in einem Spiegel,
der einen anderen Spiegel widerspiegelt.
Spiegelung hinter Spiegelung
bis ins Unendliche.

Alles ist nur ein Traum
in einem Traum,
in dem dir träumt,
daß du träumst.

Bis der Tod den Spiegel zerschlägt
und den Träumenden weckt.

———

ERNST SCHÖNWIESE

(1905–)

Born in Vienna, a critic, translator, and literary savant there, Ernst Schönwiese until recently served as head of the literary department of ORF (Austrian state radio). Schönwiese is today known as a traditional poet and the author of the definitive history of Viennese writing between 1930 and 1980, on which Schönwiese himself had a shaping influence. From 1935 to 1936, and again for seven years after the war, he edited the influential *Das Silberboot* [The silver boat], a literary journal which in the postwar years printed the international literature that had been prohibited by the Nazis. *Das Silberboot* thus played an important part in shaping the Austrian writing which followed. Since 1952, when *Das Silberboot* ceased publication, Schönwiese continued to exert his influence as a respected literary critic; in 1980 he published a history of Viennese literature between 1930 and 1980.

Schönwiese first published his poems in 1935, in *Patmos,* a collection of the works of younger Austrian poets. He went into exile during the Second World War and his poems were proscribed, but he returned to Vienna in 1945 and began his postwar career as a poet with *Der Siebenfarbige Regenbogen* [The seven-colored rainbow] (1947), and over the next two decades published nearly a dozen collections, including *Geheimnisvolles Ballspiel* [Secret games] of 1964 and *Odysseus und der Alchimist* [Odysseus and the alchemist] of 1968. Schönwiese's poems often reflect his tradition-oriented, religious, and mystical nature. Schönwiese was president of the Austrian P.E.N. Club from 1973 to 1978.

———

Everything is only a reflection
in a mirror
that reflects another mirror.
Reflection behind reflection
into infinity.

Everything is only a dream
in a dream
in which you dream
that you're dreaming.

Until death breaks the mirror
and wakes the dreamer.

———

Was in deinem Herzen so mächtig pocht,
ist der Mensch, der du wirklich bist.
Du hältst ihn gefangen.
Unablässig schlägt er gegen die Tür seines Kerkers.
Laß ihn frei!

────────

Wenn jemand gestorben ist,
werden im Haus die Spiegel verhängt.
Denn in der ungreifbaren Tiefe des Spiegels
lebt er ja jetzt,
und es könnte dich töten,
würdest du dort ihm begegnen
und das Geheimnis plötzlich erraten,
das der Tote jetzt weiß.

────────

Warum nennen wir Nacht,
was kommen wird, nach diesem Leben?
Es ist der Tag
und in seinem Licht
werden wir uns dieses Dunkels nicht mehr erinnern.

Wir sprechen von Tod,
als wüßten wir nicht,
wie viele tot sind, obwohl sie noch leben.

gewiß:
auch dort hält uns noch Schlaf umfangen.
Aber wie anders werden wir träumen!

What so strongly beats in your heart
is the being you really are.
You hold it prisoner.
It continually knocks against the door of its prison.
Free it!

———

When someone dies
mirrors are covered in the house.
For now he lives
in the inconceivable depth of mirrors,
and it could kill you
were you to meet him there
and suddenly discover the secret
known only to the dead.

———

Why do we call night
that which comes after life?
Day is what it is,
and we'll no longer remember
this darkness in its light.

We speak of death
as if we didn't know
how many who still live are dead.

To be sure,
sleep continues to embrace us there.
But how different our dreams will be!

Vor Nacht

Blutroter Ball im Milchhimmel—
wer warf ihn?
Wer hascht danach?
Wer spielt mit Blut?
Wer dürstet nach himmlischer Milch?

Wer löst das Rätsel halb
und löscht sein Seelenlicht,
wer errät es vor Nacht,
eh sein blutiger Kopf
in den Sand
vor goldne Sandalen rollt—
wer wendet den dunklen Spruch?

———

Vom Brotlaib Leben
brach ich die Kruste Treue,
brach sie,
hart und heiß
und aß.

Eisig teilte
das Trennungsmesser
Schnitte auf Schnitte mir zu,
schmerzgewürzt,
in Trauer getaucht.

HEDWIG KATSCHER

(1 8 9 8 –   )

Hedwig Katscher, who came to poetry late, began as a scientist, studying physics and mathematics at the University of Vienna. She left Austria in 1930 but returned in 1953 and has since published three collections of poetry—*Flutumdunkelt* [Dark flood] (1964), *Zwischen Herzschlag und Staub* [Between heartbeat and dust] (1969), and *Steinzeit* [Stone age] (1977). Her poems often reflect the mathematician's love for order, symmetry, and unity. Katscher is a member of the Austrian P.E.N. Club.

Before Night

Blood-red ball in the milky sky—
who threw it there?
who would catch it?
who plays with blood?
who thirsts for heavenly milk?

Who can half-solve this puzzle
and extinguish the soul's light?
who can guess it before nightfall?
before his bloody head
rolls in the sand
in front of golden sandals—
who can avert this dark curse?

———

From the bread of life
I broke the crust of faith,
broke it,
hard and hot,
and ate.

The bread-knife
cut it coldly,
slice after slice for me,
seasoned with pain,
dipped in sadness.

Ich brach und hielt,
hielt fest,
hielt mich an Treue und Trennung,
Zehrung
zugeteilt
vom warmen Brotlaib Leben
in wegloser Wildnis.

———

Deine Leidenskerze
brennt so grell,
daß sich meine Augen schließen

Auferlegt dem zarten Wachs
die Flamme,
einverleibt der peinigende Docht.

Deiner Leidenskerze weißes Licht
schmelzt das Siegel meiner Lider,
brennt in meinen Augen.

Und ich sehe,
sehe deine stillen Augen
meine fragen.
Und mein Blick erblindet.
Antwortlos.

Der Baum

Sie haben den Baum gefällt,
den atmenden Turm zertrümmert,
den Wuchs zum Himmel verwüstet,
die immergrüne Flamme ausgelöscht.

Sie haben der Erde die Wurzel entrissen,
dem Licht den Wipfel entwendet.

Sie haben's getan.

I broke it and held it,
held fast,
held on to faith and parting,
gnawed at
my share
of the warm bread of life
in the pathless wilderness.

———

Your candle of suffering
burns so brightly
that my eyes close.

The flame's infliction
on the soft wax
consumes the tormented wick.

Your candle's white light
melts the seal of my lids
and burns into my eyes.

And I see,
I see your calm eyes
question mine.
And my glance is blinded.
There is no answer.

The Tree

They have felled the tree,
demolished the breathing tower,
destroyed the object that grew toward the sky,
extinguished the evergreen flame.

They have torn the roots from the earth,
stolen its crown from the light.

They have done it.

The Generation of the War

Bei Tag

Hasenfell-Himmel. Noch immer
schreibt eine deutliche Schwinge.

Auch ich, erinnere dich,
Staub-
farbene, kam
als ein Kranich.

———————

Schwarzerde, schwarze
Erde du, Stunden-
mutter
Verzweiflung:

"PAUL CELAN"

(1920 – 1970)

"Paul Celan," or Paul Antschel, is certainly one of the most important of the postwar European poets. Born a German-speaking Jew in Chernowitz (Cernauti) in Bukovina (then Rumania, now a part of the Soviet Union) in 1920, he was displaced early. Celan was forced to abandon medical studies in Tours before the war, so he returned to his home and undertook the study of Romance languages. After the occupation of Bukovina, Celan spent three years in a labor camp before being allowed to resume his academic work.

After the war Celan made his way to Bucharest, where he published his first poems in German in 1947. Then in the next year he emigrated to Paris, where he studied German and linguistics. Becoming a French citizen, he lectured at the École Normale Supérieure. In 1970, after a distinguished literary career, Paul Celan committed suicide by drowning.

Influenced by Rilke and the French surrealists, Celan, with his varied linguistic background, was centrally obsessed with the horrors of the Jewish extermination. His first collection, published in Bucharest in 1947, contained "Todesfuge," the poem about that extermination which made his reputation. Gradually his poems became shorter, more "word-obsessed," and as he progressed Celan became conscious of "a strong inclination to remain silent."

His collections of poetry are too numerous to list here, and our sample cannot begin to represent his work. A good collection of his poems in English translation was published by Penguin in 1972. Celan's collected poems (*Gedichte*) appeared in two volumes in 1975. In 1980 Michael Hamburger translated a representative collection of Celan's poems into English in *Paul Celan: Poems* (New York: Persea, 1980). Celan's poetry has been widely discussed by critics in English as well as in other languages.

During the Day

Rabbit-fur sky. A clearly defined
wing still writes.

I too, do you remember,
dust-
colored, came
as a crane.

————

You black, black
earth, mother
of hours,
despair.

Ein aus der Hand und ihrer
Wunde dir Zu-
geborenes schließt
deine Kelche.

Erratisch

Die Abende graben sich dir
unters Aug. Mit der Lippe auf-
gesammelte Silben—schönes,
lautloses Rund—
helfen dem Kriechstern
in ihre Mitte. Der Stein,
schläfennah einst, tut sich hier auf:

bei allen
versprengten
Sonnen, Seele,
warst du, im Äther.

————

Einiges Hand-
ähnliche, finster,
kam mit den Gräsern:

Rasch—Verzweiflungen, ihr
Töpfer!—, rasch
gab die Stunde den Lehm her, rasch
war die Träne gewonnen—:

noch einmal, mit bläulicher Rispe,
umstand es uns, dieses
Heute.

————

Es ist nicht mehr
diese
zuweilen mit dir
in die Stunde gesenkte
Schwere. Es ist
eine andre.

Something born to you
of the hand and its wound
closes
your calyx.

Erratic

The evenings bury themselves
under your eye. Syllables collected
by the lips—beautiful,
soundlessly round—
aid the creeping star
in their midst. The stone,
once close to the temple, discloses itself:

during all
the explosions
of suns, my soul,
there you were, in the ether.

————

Something dark
resembling a hand
came with the grasses:

Quickly—there was despair, you
potters!—, the hour quickly
provided the clay, quickly
the tear was achieved;

once again, with its bluish tufts,
this thing was all around us,
this today.

————

It is no longer
that heaviness
which, at times, with you
sank into the hour.
It is a different one.

Es ist das Gewicht, das die Leere zurückhält,
die mit-
ginge mit dir.
Es hat, wie du, keinen Namen. Vielleicht
seid ihr dasselbe. Vielleicht
nennst auch du mich einst
so.

It is the weight that keeps back the emptiness
which went along
with you.
Like you, it has no name. Perhaps
you are one and the same. Perhaps
at times you speak this way
of me.

———

Ein Flügelpaar schreibt,
sich faltend, sich
öffnend—
wär' es
das Nun?

Unverwirrt und frei,
mit dem Herzen lesbare Echospuren,
aller Dinge und Sterne
Winkel
stehen aufs neu' zueinander.

MAX HÖLZER

(1915–   )

Max Hölzer was born in Graz and studied law at the University of Jena; he has followed a career as an attorney and later as a judge. But Max Hölzer is also one of the important Austrian poets of his generation.

Hölzer emigrated to Paris as a young man and lived there for a time as a freelance writer. In Paris he was closely associated with another Austrian emigré, Paul Celan. They lived near one another and together translated their own poetry and that of a number of French poets. Hölzer was deeply influenced in these years by the French surrealist poets, especially by André Breton, whose poems were among those he translated. Like other surrealists Hölzer in his own poetry experimented with *automatisme,* with montage techniques, and with other innovative methods of composition.

Later Hölzer lived in Madrid and Frankfurt, where he edited *Surrealistische Publikationen* (1950–1952); he was thus the first to introduce the surrealists to German readers. He translated a number of French poets into German—in addition to Breton, Nathalie Serraute, George Bataille, and Pierre Reverdy among them. Hölzer has also written on various poets, including Paul Valéry.

Hölzer's own poetry has appeared in several collections, the most famous being perhaps *Der Doppelgänger* [The double] (1959). His first book was *Entstehung eines Sternbilds* [The beginning of a constellation] (1958); later there appeared *Nigredo* (1962) and *Gesicht ohne Gesicht* [Sight without sight] (1964), *Lunariae* (poems in French, 1972), and in 1976 *Mare occidentalis, Das verborgene Licht, Chrysopöe* [Western sea, The secret light, Chrysopöe]. Hölzer is the indispensable presence in the establishment of surrealism in German and Austrian poetry.

A pair of wings writes
folding,
opening—
was it
the here and now?

Unconfused and free,
with the heart discernible by its echo,
all things, the stars,
stand in a new relationship
to one another.

Opium

Wälder
um plüschgedeckten Tisch
dessen Weiße wächst
fern meiner Hand—

Wer zieht aus dem Schatten
leuchtenden Frauenarm
gewohnt ins Weiße
hinunter

———

Tische. Tisch. Hier
weht das Scheinen hervor,
unsichtbar.

Fühle die Wangen,
schau nicht auf, ver-
tief' dich.

Über
unberührbarem Wolkenverzicht,
in der Morgennacht,
verglüht
eine Gemme.

Unberührbar

Ein Vogel schwirrt gegen das Fenster.
Er schlägt an die Scheibe
die die Brust des Verlassenen teilt.

Kostüm aus Sonne und Nebel
das der Zug auf den Marschen steppte
jenen Morgen—
leg es ab.

Leg es ab.
Töte den Vogel.
—Doch es liegt so eng an
wie der Laut nicht seinem Mund.

Opium

Forests
around a plush-covered table
whose whiteness grows
far from my hand—

Whoever draws from the shadow
a woman's radiant arm
becomes accustomed to the whiteness
below

———

Tables. Table. Here
the luster breaks through
invisibly.

Feel the cheeks,
don't look up, sink
deep into yourself.

Above the intangible renunciation of the clouds
in the night of early morning
a jewel
glows its last.

Intangible

A bird whirrs against the window.
It beats against the pane
which shares the breast of the abandoned one.

Costume of sun and fog
quilted by the currents on the marshes
one morning—
take it off.

Take it off.
Kill the bird.
But it fits so snugly
like a sound not from its mouth.

Copyright

Wieviel
Jahre
nach
Gottes
Tod
erlöschen
seine
ausländischen
und
deutschen
Urheberrechte

ERICH FRIED

(1921 –   )

Born in Vienna, Erich Fried emigrated to London after his father was killed by the Gestapo. Fried has lived there since. He has worked as a translator of British writers, notably Dylan Thomas, but also T. S. Eliot, Graham Greene, J. M. Synge, and even Shakespeare, and he worked for a time on the German service of BBC, although in 1968 he resigned for political reasons. As a writer and poet Fried is associated with a dry intellectual firmness and an intense political commitment; he is troubled not only by the Jewish persecutions in World War II but by more recent events, among them Vietnam.

Fried began his literary career in 1940 and since 1944 has produced nearly a dozen collections of poems. Like many of his Austrian contemporaries his political concerns are mixed with a Wittgensteinian love of language, its manipulation, and its magic. But Fried is also a love poet; his single novel, *Ein Soldat und ein Mädchen* [A soldier and a girl] (1960), which tells the story of the love of a Jewish-American soldier during the occupation for a former concentration camp warden under sentence of death, manifests Fried's curiously ironic fusion of awarenesses. In the 1970s Fried's poetry has appeared in *Höre, Israel* [Hear, O Israel] (1974) and *Gegengift* [Antidote] (1974). He has recently participated with Ralph Mannheim in the collection of the poems of Bertolt Brecht, and Fried's own poems have appeared in English translation in three collections: *Last Honors* (1968), *On Pain of Seeing* (1969), and *100 Poems without a Country* (1978). Fried is a member of the Graz Authors' Collective.

Copyright

How
many
years
after
God's
death
will
his
foreign
and
German
rights
expire

Seifenblasen

Ich klammerte mich
an einen Strohhalm
und blies
Politiker
Generäle
und Polizisten

Sie schillerten
aufgeblasen
in allen Farben
aber sie platzten
sowie man sie
berührte

Ein Polizist
dem ich das sagte
ohne ihn zu berühren
berührte mich
mit seinem Schlagstock
so daß ich platzte

Vorteile einer Nacktkultur

Die nackte
Angst
scheint jetzt
leichter
zu tragen

als bisher
in ihren schweren
Kleidern
die sie
verhüllten

Sprachlos

Warum schreibst du
noch immer
Gedichte
obwohl du

Soap Bubbles

I grasped at
a straw
and blew bubbles of
politicians
generals
and policemen

They shimmered
puffed up
in all colors
but they burst
when they
were touched

A policeman
that I told this to
without touching him
touched me
with his truncheon
so that I burst

Advantages of Nudism

Naked fear
now seems
easier
to bear

than
it used to be
with heavy
clothing
covering it

Speechless

Why
do you still
write poems
although you know

mit dieser Methode
immer nur
Minderheiten erreichst

fragen mich Freunde
ungeduldig darüber
daß sie mit ihren Methoden
immer nur
Minderheiten erreichen

und ich weiß
keine Antwort
für sie

that you can only
reach a minority
with this method

my friends ask me
impatient that
they can only
reach a minority
with their methods

and I can't
give them
an answer

―――――

ein wasserblauer baum
schlägt hoch
wie ein brunnen

morgendämmerung und strahl
ein gespannter bogen
der noch nicht
zum klingen
gebracht ist

eisfest
wie verborgenes korn

H. C. ARTMANN

(1921 –)

Born in Vienna, the son of a shoemaker and without a formal education to speak of, H[ans] C[arl] Artmann is today a delightful, linguistically delighted, and thoroughly amazing polyglot poet. He takes great pleasure in languages, whether English, Celtic, or the dialect German of his region and his city. He also shows the influence of dada and has been one of its leading advocates in postwar Austrian poetry.

Artmann—with Friedrich Achleitner, Konrad Bayer, and Gerhard Rühm—was one of the more important poets of the Vienna Group in the 1950s; later he appeared as a reigning presence in the Graz Group. Artmann has always been antiestablishment; he has sought to expose the dark center of the golden Viennese heart in plays like *kein pfeffer für czermak* [no pepper for czermak] (1954). At the same time he has done much to reestablish the dialect tradition in Austrian poetry after the war, first with *med ana schwoazzn dintn* [with black ink] (1958), one of the most popular books of poetry written in German since the war, and a year later, in collaboration with Achleitner and Rühm, in *Hosn, rosn, baa [Britches, blooms, bones].*

Artmann has spent many years abroad. He has lived in Malmö and Berlin, was for a time more or less based in Brittany, where he followed his interest in Celtic poetry, and now lives in Salzburg and travels much of each year. His own work shows many influences and gives evidence of wide reading—of Rilke, Trakl, Lorca, even the English nonsense poet Edward Lear. His poems, some of them "sense-free sound poems," combine dialect, parody, and pastiche to produce an often profoundly serious statement. Artmann has over twenty books to his credit. One of his real delights is the curiously titled German-language collection *The Best of H. C. Artmann* (1970). In 1969 Gerald Bisinger collected Artmann's poetical work of the previous two decades in a book entitled *ein lilienweißer brief aus lincolnshire* [A lilly-white letter from Lincolnshire].

---

a water-blue tree
rises high
like a fountain

daybreak and a light-beam
a tightened bow
that has not yet
drawn
sound

ice-hard
like choice schnapps

ungeküßt wie ein mund
dem ein frischer traum
vor den lippen steht
eine schöne bitte
noch nicht aufzuwachen

noch nicht jetzt
noch nicht

———

die sonne ist ein neues haus
du schreibst es
es ist morgen
wir halten unsre hände durch
die offnen fenster

die grille stellt ihr uhrwerk
du schreibst es
es ist morgen
der tag legt ein blaues kleid
in unsrem garten zurecht

oh wie ist die rose kühl noch
du schreibst es
es ist morgen
die falter hüllen ihre flügel
in seidenpapier noch

jedes wort kommt aus der rose
du schreibst es
es ist morgen
wie schön die blätter so blatt
um blatt zu erwarten

ein genau gehälfteter apfel
du schreibst es
es ist morgen
vielleicht daß der lerche ihr
flug ihn wieder bindet

———

unkissed like a mouth
with a fresh dream
on its lips
a beautiful wish
not to wake up yet

not quite yet
not yet

————

the sun is a new house
you write it
it is morning
we reach out
through the open windows

the cricket resets its clock
you write it
it is morning
day lays a blue dress
neatly in our garden

oh how cool the rose still is
you write it
it is morning
butterflies are still wrapping
their wings in silk paper

each word comes from the rose
you write it
it is morning
how wonderful to wait for
the leaves leaf by leaf

an apple in two halves exactly
you write it
it is morning
perhaps the lark's flight
will put it together again

————

immer die vögel
des himmels

der lange blaue
strand zaudert
silbern im morgen

die rote sonne
beginnt
schönes emblem
auf der brust
eines engels

küß du mich
mit deinem mund
tagnahe

wie ein falke
wie ein ziel
wie ein ferner
weißer punkt

wie eine flagge
weitab
im frühlicht

immer die vögel
des himmels

————

für uns beide
peitscht die trommel
den dampf
konvulsion
ist uns beschieden
von vorneherein
daß du glaubtest
dies rasseln käme aus
dem abgrund des mittags
oder aus der reliquie
vergorener sonne . . .
mehr oder weniger

always birds
in the sky

the long blue
beach lingers
silver in the morning

the red sun
rises
a bright emblem
on the breast
of an angel

kiss me
with your mouth
close as day

like a falcon
like a target
like a distant
white spot

like a flag
far off
in the morning light

always birds
in the sky

———

the drum
whips up steam
for both of us
convulsion
was assigned to us
right from the beginning
so that you thought
this rattling
came from
the depths of noon
or from the relic
of a rotten sun . . .
more or less

als ganze bejahung
werden wir nie erreichen
hierorts . . .

———

a rosn
fümf rosn
dreizzen rosn
a lilibutanarin
fümf lilibutanarina
dreizzen lilibutanarina

a lilibutanarin und a rosn
fümf lilibutanarina und fümf rosn
dreizzen lilibutanarina und dreizzen rosn

a dode lilibutanarin
fümf dode lilibutanarina
dreizzen dode lilibutanarina

a dode rosn
fümf dode rosn
dreizzen dode rosn
a dode lilibutanarin
und a dode rosn
fümf dode lilibutanarina
und fümf dode rosn
dreizzen dode lilibutanarina
und dreizzen dode rosn

rosn
zoen
lilibutanarina
und
da dod

than complete affirmation
is unattainable for us
here . . .

———

a rose
five roses
thirteen roses
a female midget
five female midgets
thirteen female midgets

a female midget and a rose
five female midgets and five roses
thirteen female midgets and thirteen roses

a dead female midget
five dead female midgets
thirteen dead female midgets

a dead rose
five dead roses
thirteen dead roses
a dead female midget
and a dead rose
five dead female midgets
and five dead roses
thirteen dead female midgets
and thirteen dead roses

roses
numbers
female midgets
and death

Zugehörig

Meine schwarzen Pferde,
die ich weiden sehe,
die für mich davonweiden
ins Holz, in die Algen,
meine Tiere,
die mich hindern
zu bestehen,
die entzwei reiten,
was kommt,
die das kennen,
weil sie meine sind
und sonst nichts.

Gebirgsrand

Denn was täte ich,
wenn die Jäger nicht wären, meine Träume,
die am Morgen
auf der Rückseite der Gebirge
niedersteigen, im Schatten.

ILSE AICHINGER

(1921 –)

Ilse Aichinger was born in Vienna in 1921. Soon after the war her World War II novel, *Die größere Hoffnung* [The greater hope] (1948, translated in 1963 as *Herod's Children*) gained her an international reputation as a writer of fiction. More recently her fiction has shown the influence of Franz Kafka and has become symbolical, surreal, curiously ironic. These characteristics are manifest in *Der Gefesselte* [The bound man] (1956), *Eliza, Eliza* (1965), and *Meine Sprache und ich* [My language and myself] (1978), all collections of short stories. Many of these stories have been translated into English.

Ilse Aichinger, however, is also distinguished as a writer of radio plays, of "dialogues" (a genre she invented), and of poetry. Her best known radio plays were *Knöpfe* [Buttons] (1953) and *Auckland* (1969); her most recent volume of poetry is *Verschenkter Rat* [Advice given] (1978). Aichinger's *Selected Poetry and Prose* appeared in English in 1983.

Belonging

My black horses
that I see grazing,
grazing away for me
into the wood, into the seaweed,
my animals
that keep me
from being
that trample under foot
whatever appears
know nothing but this
because they are mine
and nothing else.

Edge of the Mountain

So what would I do
if those hunters, my dreams, were no more,
who in the morning
climb down
the far side of the mountain
into the shadow.

Spät

Holzfarben
und die Kerze
rostrot im Schatten entzündet,
weht der Wind
durch die Schneise,
lockt sich die Sonne hinweg.

Wenn erst
Backhaus und Scheune
sich nach dem Niedergang strecken,
fängt der Himmel
die Stämme,
rostet der Schnee vor dem Jahr.

Ausgedacht

Wenn die Foltern gebündelt sind,
geh ich nach Bayonne
und schieb mich durch die Gitter,
die ich meine,
und hör den Gips dort knistern,
den ich wollte,
wie ich wollte,
ohne ihn zu streicheln
und solang ich will.

Late

Wood colors
and the candle
burning rust red in the shadow,
the wind blows
through the glade,
the sun is lured away.

When the shadows
of bakery and barn
stretch out in the sunset
the sky catches
the tree trunks
and the snow rusts before its time.

Thought Out

When the torture racks are put away
I'll go to Bayonne
and squeeze through the bars
as I intended to
and hear the plaster crack
as I wanted to
the way I wanted to
without touching it
for as long as I want to.

Miserere

Schuldig sind wir geworden
wie die Robbenfänger im ewigen Eis.

Für uns wird kein Platz im Paradies sein.
es wimmelt von Robben,
ängstlich hüten die Engel die Fische.

In der Finsternis, in der Kälte
suchen wir nach seligen Orten,
wo uns ein tranloses Feuer wärmt.

———

Vollstreckt ist
die Enthauptung der Sonnenblume.

Mähdrescherzeit.
Sie sagen, es leuchtet nicht mehr.
In den Bettelsack
mit den grauen Kernen!

Unscheinbar birgt sich der Zukunft
das Öl und das Licht.

"CHRISTINE BUSTA"

(1915–   )

Christine Dimt, or "Christine Busta," was born in Vienna in modest circumstances in 1915. In 1936 because of serious illness she was forced to abandon her university studies, and four years later she married the musician Maximillian Dimt (Dimt has been among the missing in Russia since 1944). Christine Busta served as municipal librarian for the city of Vienna until her recent retirement.

A religious poet who frequently employs biblical phrasings, Christine Busta has identified her "basic theme" as "the transformation of fear, terror, and guilt into joy, love, and redemption." Her poems were first collected in 1950, and she has continued actively to write poems, both for adults and for children, ever since. Christine Busta's *Der Regenbaum* [The rain tree] (1951), an early collection of poems, was republished in 1977. A more recent collection, *Salzgärten* [Salt Gardens], appeared in 1975. Busta is a member of the Austrian P.E.N. Club.

Miserere

We have assumed guilt
like seal-hunters on eternal ice.

There's no place in Paradise for us:
it's teeming with seals,
and angels anxiously guard the fish.

In the darkness, in the cold,
we search for holy places
where we will be warmed
by a fire not stoked with fish oil.

———

They've cut down
the sunflower.

Time for mowing.
They say it no longer shines.
In the beggar's sack
with its gray seeds.

The future conceals
oil and light.

———

Ein schwarzer Engel
wird kommen und sagen
«Verleugnet hat seine Farbe der Schnee,
die Schwäne verfluchen ihr weißes Gefieder,
das Linnen schwört, eure Haut ist fleckig,
die Milch der Kühe verfärbt sich mit Blut. . . .»

Dürre

In rissigen Lettern die Heilige Schrift
auf den Böden der Sahelzone:
Gott ist Wasser,
Gott ist Brot,
und das Wort
ist Knochen geworden.

Unser Schmerzenskind

So herz- und hautnah
wir liegen,
immer liegt
zwischen dir und mir
unser
Leben ohne einander.

Rauhreif

Alles ist Blüte geworden,
Frostblüte
Nebelgedicht.

Mit gläsernen Zweigen
läutet der Weg
ins weiße Exil der Raben.

———

An angel in black
will appear and say,
"Snow has denied its color,
swans curse their white feathers,
the linen swears that your skin is spotted,
cows give milk colored with blood. . . ."

Drought

The Holy Scriptures in cracked letters
on the surface of the Sahel Zone:
God is water,
God is bread,
and the Word
has become bone.

Our Child of Pain

Although we lie
heart- and skin-
close,
always between you and me
lies
our life without each other.

Hoarfrost

Everything blooms:
frost-blossom
fog-poem.

The path
to the white exile of ravens
rings with glassy branches.

———————

Durch die stählerne Luft
einsam
schraubt sich ein Vogel
hinweg von der Erde.
Ich vermisse den Mond
und die Schläge meines Herzens,
während der Wind im Segenbaum wühlt,
nach verlorener Richtung,
Morgen—wenn es die Sonne will,
wird mein Leib sich wieder erwärmen dürfen.
Paarweise werden die Tauben dann
vom Himmel nieder zur Erde tauchen
und mein Herz zurück in die Hoffart,
die Richtung der Unzahl.

———————

Hinter dem Rücken der hiesigen Zeit
hab ich der andern, der doppeltgehörnten
vogelfüßige Zeichen gemacht,
bis die Glorie herfand.
Wie Waisen müssen wir atmen,
unauffällig und räuberisch,

"CHRISTINE LAVANT"

(1915 – 1973)

Christine Hahrnig (née Thonhauser), who wrote under a pseudonym taken from the name of her native valley in Carinthia, was born in Gross-Edling, the ninth child of a miner. Partially deaf and blind from birth, she first earned her living by knitting. At the age of twenty-four she married a sixty-year-old artist. She spent most of her life in her native valley and died in Wolfsberg.

Christine Lavant began publishing her stories and her devoutly Catholic and mystical poetry before the war, but it was *Die Bettlerschale* [The beggar's cup] of 1956 that made her reputation as a poet. In 1962 another collection, *Pfauenschrei* [Peacock's cry], appeared, and there have been several others. In 1964 Lavant was awarded the Trakl Prize; today she is certainly one of Austria's most widely read poets. A collection of Christine Lavant's various writings, including her poems, entitled *Kunst wie meine ist nur verstummeltes Leben* [Art like mine is only distorted life], appeared in 1978.

————

Through the steely air
alone
a bird twists
away from the earth.
I miss the moon
and my heartbeats
while the wind ransacks the blessed tree,
having lost all direction.
Tomorrow, if the sun wills it,
my body can warm itself again.
And doves will descend in pairs
from Heaven to Earth,
and my heart will regain its pride,
the path toward infinity.

————

Behind the back of our time
I have made bird-foot signs
to the other one, the double-horned one
until Glory has found its way here.
Like orphans we must breathe
like inconspicuous thieves

bis wir die Zehrung beisammen haben
für den Flug in die Freude.
Doch die Erde hat eine knöcherne Hand
und Fundevögel auf jedem Knochen,
ihre pfauenäugige Leimrute lockt
meine Augen zurück in das Elend.

———

Endlos schreit vom Hohlweg herüber
und unausstehlich die Regenkröte.
Der späte Mond und mein Herz
gleichen an diesem Oktoberabend
einem aufgerissenen Wespenkrug.
Lautlos gleiten die schwarzen Schiffe
hastiger Vögel am Fenster vorbei
und erschrecken mich und die Abendspinne.
Halbfertig über Stirne und Augen
hängt mir das dünne Gewebe des Schlafes.
Bald wird es schwer von meinen Ängsten sein,
denn unerträglich dünkt mich das Zeichen
des aufgerissenen Wespenkruges,
den der Wind jetzt vom Schuppendach bläst.

———

Du hast mich aus aller Freude geholt.
Aber ich werde dennoch genau,
ganz genau, nur so lange darunter leiden,
als es mir selbst gefällig ist, Herr.
Du hast mich im Zustand der wildesten Hoffart
und des zornigsten Mutes vor dir.
Heb deine Hand und schlage mich nieder,
ich werde dann nur um so höher springen,
und du wirst mich ewig vor Augen haben,
den kleinen, roten, zornigen Ball.
Jede Stelle wirft mich zu dir zurück,
weil du mich von jener einzigen Stelle,
wo ich Herz war und freudig und weich wie ein Vogel,
wegholtest, um mich zusammenzuballen
und ins ewige Leiden zu werfen.

until we have gathered the provisions
for the flight into joy.
But the earth has a bony hand
and each bone is a new bird;
its peacock-eyed lime twig lures
my eyes back to misery.

————

From the sunken road a rain frog croaks
intolerably and uninterruptedly.
The late moon and my heart
on this October evening
are like a hornet's nest ripped open.
Silently moving like black ships
the quick birds fly by my window
and frighten the night spider and me.
Half-finished over my head and eyes
hangs the thin web of sleep.
Soon it will be heavy with my fears
for it seems impossible to bear the sign
of the ripped-open hornet's nest
that the wind now blows from the barn roof.

————

You have taken me from all joy.
But in spite of that, I will only suffer
for just as long, for exactly as long
as I want to, Lord.
I stand before You in a state
of the wildest pride and angriest courage.
Lift Your hand and strike me down,
and I'll jump all the higher
and You'll have me before You forever,
a small, red, angry ball.
Each place bounces me back to You
because You took me from the only place
where I was all heart and happy and soft as a bird,
transported me, rolled me up into a ball,
and cast me into eternal suffering.

Träume!
Deine Stunde ist es nicht

Träume! Deine Stunde ist es nicht.
Deine Stunde wird wie gestern sein,
wenn du aufwachst am Morgen in der fremden Stadt,
wenn du aufwachst in der fremden Heimat,
wenn du aufwachst unter einem Namen,
der Verzweiflung heißt, vielleicht Geduld.

Träume! Noch ist es zu früh, zu spät.
Noch ist nicht die Zeit der vielen Sonnen,
nicht die Zeit der Coniferen,
noch die Zeit des Honigsammelns für die Bienen,
nicht die Zeit zum Hochzeitsflug.

Paris ist eine Roulette

Paris ist eine Roulette. Du mußt selber Dich setzen.
Wessen Nummer nicht zieht, geht schnell in die Seine.
Davor haben Bouquinisten ihre Wälle gebaut,
und statt ins Wasser zu springen
liest mancher Verlaine. Im Vorübergehn.

HERBERT ZAND

(1 9 2 3 – 1 9 7 0)

Born in Bad Aussee the son of a farmer, Herbert Zand served in the army in World War II and was seriously wounded on the Russian front. After the war he worked as a publisher's helper, later as a writer. He began his career as a novelist, publishing his first novel in 1947. Zand had written three others by 1961, when *Erben des Feuers* [Heritage of fire], a work sharply critical of postwar Austria, appeared.

Zand's reputation as a poet was established with *Die Glaskugel* [The crystal ball], a collection which appeared in 1953. Zand died as a result of his wartime injuries in 1970. His *Gesammelte Werke* [Complete works] were compiled and edited by Wolfgang Kraus in a six-volume edition published by Europaverlag in 1973. The poems in this anthology were taken from the volume of that collection entitled *Aus zerschossenem Sonnengeflecht* [Out of the sun's battered plaits].

Dreams, Your Time Hasn't Come

Dreams, your time hasn't come.
Your time will be like yesterday,
when you wake up one morning in a strange city,
when you wake up in a strange home,
when you wake up with a name
that's called despair, or perhaps patience.

Dreams, it's still too early, too late.
It isn't yet the time of many suns,
not the time of the hemlocks;
now is the time for bees to collect honey,
not the time for marriage-flight.

Paris Is a Game of Roulette

Paris is a game of roulette.
You must wager yourself.
If your number doesn't come up,
you'll end up in the Seine fast enough.
To prevent that, secondhand booksellers
have built their embankments;
Instead of jumping into the water
some read Verlaine. In passing.

Die Schere der Einsamkeit schneidet
ihre Schattenrisse aus der Nacht.
Jeder von ihnen leidet,
und keiner hat Acht, wie die Schere schneidet:
krumm manchmal und schief. . . .
Manch einer hat auch gedacht,
die Seine sei nicht tief.
Dabei ist kein Fluß tiefer als
die Seine und keiner so unbewacht
wie sie. Trotz Verlaine.

Setz deinen Schatten aufs Rad,
            verspiel die Seele.

Mein ganzes Leben lang

Mein ganzes Leben lang
habe ich versucht,
ein paar Dinge zu begreifen:
die ruhige Zuversicht,
die Kraft der Liebe,
die Kraft des freien Entschlusses
und die Kraft des Wortes,
wenn es gebraucht wird.

Ich weiß, daß es die Freude gibt
und daß es die Trauer gibt,
und ich falte die Zeitungen,
und ich schließe die Bücher,
sie berichten zu wenig.

Sie nennen die Dinge mit Namen.
Ich bin jetzt den anderen auf der Spur,
die keinen Namen haben,
zwischen Freude und Trauer,
zwischen Glück und Schmerz,
allen noch namenlosen Dingen,
die stumm sind wie am Anfang der Welt.

Die Rehe

Schöner sind sie als Haustiere,
zarter auch,
ohne Zutrauen, dazu geschaffen,

The scissors of loneliness cut
their shadowy slashes in the night.
Each one of them suffers,
and no one notices
how the scissors cut
sometimes crookedly and obliquely. . . .
Some of them doubted that the Seine was deep.
But no river is deeper
and none so unguarded.
In spite of Verlaine.

Bet your shadow on the wheel,
   let your soul be the stakes.

My Whole Life Long

My whole life long
I've tried
to understand a few things:
calm confidence,
the power of love,
the power of free choice,
and the power of the word
when used.

I know that there is happiness,
and that there is sadness,
and I fold up papers,
and I close books,
they don't tell me enough.

They call things by name.
I'm now on the track of other things,
that have no name,
between happiness and sadness,
between joy and pain,
all the nameless things
which are as mute as at time's beginning.

Deer

They are more beautiful than domestic animals,
and more delicate,
without trust, born

ein Leben lang auf der Flucht zu sein,
im Schnee zu erfrieren
beim Sonnenaufgang im Januar.

Manchmal, auf Schlitten, werden sie in das Dorf gefahren.
Die Köpfe hängen nach unten. In vollendeter,
schrecklicher Schönheit ruhen sie aus.
Die Kinder scheuen vor diesem Bild
als wären Dämonen im Spiel, furchtbarer noch
als die Riesen der Märchen, und könnten
ihr Leben verderben. Die Frauen
wenden sich ab. Blut. Ein Tannenzweig.
Das ist ihr Tod.

Wenn sie könnten, würden sie diese Erde verlassen
und fliehen auf andere Sterne,
wo Bäume sind ohne Zahl und mildere Winter.
Auf einsamen Wiesen würden sie gehn,
äsend im silbernen Tau beim Verblassen der Monde.
Niemals brächte der sausende Wind aus den Wäldern
Witterung von Gefahr.

to be in flight for a lifetime,
to freeze to death in the snow
at dawn in January.

Sometimes they are brought into the village on sleds.
Heads hanging down. Resting in utterly
horrible beauty.
Children turn away from this sight,
as if they were demons in a play, even more terrifying
than the giants in fairy tales, and could
ruin their lives. Women
turn away. Blood. The branch of a fir tree.
This is their death.

If they could, they would leave this earth
for other planets,
where there are countless trees and mild winters.
They would wander lonely fields
grazing in the silver dew where the moon goes pale.
And the wind rushing from the forests would never bring
the scent of danger.

Im Walde

Dreimal drei Wege und noch
einmal drei führen über den Berg.
Du mußt nur
den Abzählreim wissen,
dann kannst du auch
den dreizehnten finden.

Der führt dich nach gestern,
wo du vergessen hast, daß morgen
nichts mehr zu ändern ist.

Augustmond

Aus dem Scheunenatem
aus dem Maisfelderdunst
aus den Kastanienkronen
aus den Disteln vergessener Bahndämme
aus den Holunderzäunen

GERHARD FRITSCH

(1921 – 1969)

In his introduction to *Between Evening and Night*, the 1978 English-language collection of the poems of Gerhard Fritsch, Harry Zohn says of its author, "In the two decades after World War II he was one of the leading figures in Austrian letters. . . ." Fritsch was born in Vienna, served as a pilot during the war (*Zwischen Kirkenes und Bari* [Between Kirkenes and Bari], his first book, published in 1952, describes that experience). Taken prisoner, he escaped, and later studied at the University of Vienna, left the Communist party, and became a librarian.

Fritsch in 1959 became a freelance writer. He soon emerged as an important editor in his native city, who in his critiques and anthologies helped form a response to what he called the "stylistic dictatorship of conservatism" in Austrian letters. Fritsch was also important as a translator, translating, among others, W. H. Auden and Miroslav Krleža. He wrote for radio and published several volumes of nonfiction, but he is best known for his novels—*Moos auf den Steinen* [Moss on the stones] (1956) and *Fasching* (1967)—his stories, and his poems. Fritsch hanged himself in 1969.

Fritsch's poems appear centrally in three collections, *Lehm und Gestalt* [Clay and form] (1954), a long poem entitled *Dieses Dunkel heißt Nacht* [This darkness called night] (1955), and *Der Geisterkrug* [The ghostly jug] (1958). His prose was collected in 1974 in a posthumous edition, *Katzenmusik* [Cats' music], as were his poems, collected in 1978 as *Gesammelte Gedichte*.

In the Forest

Three times three paths and yet
three more lead over the mountain.
You must know
this counting-rhyme,
then you'll be able
to find the thirteenth.

This leads you to yesterday
where you have forgotten that, tomorrow,
nothing will be changed.

August Moon

Out of the breath of barns
out of the mist of cornfields
out of the crowns of chestnut trees
out of thistles on deserted railway embankments
out of elderberry hedges

aus den Friedhofsecken
aus dem Staub
aus dem Staub
aus dem Ozean von Staub
rollt lautlos der Mond
der riesige Kürbis
auf die Sternstraßen
der Ebene.

Von Dorf zu Dorf
bahnen ihm Hunde
den Weg.

Judas

Wenn Passion ist, muß
einer den Judas spielen. Ob
ihn das Los trifft, ob er sich gar
freiwillig meldet, ist für den Gang
der Handlung nicht wichtig. Es macht
nichts wenn er seine Rolle schlecht
beherrscht: er endet am Ast.
Wir atmen auf, diesmal
haben wir unsere Begabung
verborgen, den Judas zu spielen,
ob Passion ist
oder nicht.

Nachher

Zurückgekehrt
in ihre Matrosen-Anzüge
singen die Henker Ehre sei Gott,
den es gibt. Wir vergeben ihre Schuld
unseren Opfern. Sie haben
ihre Pflicht erfüllt wie wir,
Da gibt es nichts
zu lachen. Wir passen
in das Gewand unserer Unschuld.
Ein Wunder nur
für die Ungläubigen,
die unsere Andacht vergeblich
zu stören versuchen.

out of the corners of graveyards
out of dust
out of dust
out of an ocean of dust
the moon rolls silently
a giant pumpkin
on the starry roads
of the plain.

From village to village
dogs make way
for it.

Judas

Every passion play
must have its Judas. Whether
he's chosen by lot or whether
he volunteers is irrelevant
to the dénouement. And it doesn't
matter whether he plays his role
badly or not—he ends up on the tree.
We sigh with relief,
this time we've concealed our ability
to play Judas,
passion play
or not.

Afterward

Having put on
their sailor suits again,
hangmen sing Praise Be to God,
who exists. We forgive our victims
for their sins. They've fulfilled
their duty as we have.
This is nothing
to laugh about. The garments
of our innocence fit us.
It is a miracle
only for the unbelievers,
who fruitlessly attempt
to disrupt our prayers.

Im wirren Menschenknäuel
ein Leib,
entblößt und nackt,
entkleidet jeder
äußeren Menschenwürde,
gefoltert
von den
schwarzen Mörderpranken,
die Töten
sich zum Götzendienst
erkoren,
gehst Du den letzten
Schritt des Tages.
Die Angst
ist längst Dir aus
dem Herz gewichen.
Du trittst
mit Brüdern
und mit Schwestern
den Opfergang
mit hocherhobenem Haupte
an
und weißt Dich
Fackel;
weißt, daß Du

THOMAS SESSLER

(1915–)

Born in Berlin the son of the Austrian journalist and writer A. H. Zeiz ("Georg Fraser"), Thomas Sessler's early anti-Nazi writings led him to exile and finally to Auschwitz and Dachau. He escaped to France with the help of an American and enlisted in the American army in 1944.

After the war Sessler established himself in Vienna as a writer, editor, and publisher; he wrote for children, for radio, for the stage, and as a poet; his first collection of poems, published in 1946, was *Bienenlegende* [The fables of the bees]. Later, in 1970, he would publish his distinguished collection of poems *Unendlichkeit wird bleiben* [Infinity will remain]. In the same year his dramatic work, *Im Zeichen der Ratte* [The sign of the rat], appeared.

Curiously enough, Sessler (he writes as a journalist under the name of "Gabriel Thomas") is also the translator of *Uncle Tom's Cabin*. He is a member of the Austrian P.E.N. Club.

———

In a tangled knot of humanity
you take the last
steps of the day,
a body,
exposed and naked,
stripped of all
external dignity,
tortured
by the black murderous claws
of those
who've devoted themselves
to serving death.
Fear
left your
heart long ago.
You walk
the sacrificial path
among brothers
and sisters,
with head held high,
knowing
that you are
a torch,
knowing
that you are to be

zum ungewollten
Gottesopfer wirst,
wohl namenlos,
doch gleichsam
eingemeißelt
in unsühnbare Schuld
der Henker.

————

Ich weiß,
als hätte
es sich
in mich
eingebrannt,
als wäre es
mit heißem Blut
geschrieben,
mit Blut von Dir,
das tief
in mir
verblieben,
ich weiß
ein letztes Wort
das ich vernahm,
bevor die Nacht
erbarmend
Deinen Leib
in ihrem Schatten
barg.
Du riefst mir zu,
trotz allem
zu verzeihen.
Ob ich es kann?
Solang ich wähn',
daß hinter
jedem Biedermann
ein Mörder wohnt,
werd' ich nach
Deinem—meiner Mutter—
Henker fahnden.

————

an unintended
sacrifice to God,
nameless to be sure
but nevertheless
carved
into the unatonable guilt
of the executioners.

———————

I know it
as if I had been
branded with it,
as if it had been
written in warm blood,
in your blood
that runs
deep in me
I know
the last word
which I heard
before night
mercifully
concealed your body
in its shadows.
You called to me
to forgive
in spite of everything.
But how can I?
As long as I suspect
that every respectable
exterior
masks a murderer,
I'll be compelled
to search
for your executioner,
mother.

———————

Wenn jener Tag
uns erreicht,
jener Tag
der tödlichen Stille,
dem die Glocken
das Klingen
versagen,
der Blüte und Blume
knickt,
der die Sterne
blendet,
der den Gezeiten
Stillstand gebietet,
da die Luft
zum Sterben
sich bettet,
wird,
in angstvoller Eile
flüchtig vereint,
unserer Hände
letzter Liebesdruck
im Sog der
flammenden Garben
zerfallen.
Vermählt,
wird uns Asche
gebären.

———

Der Rauch
wird verwehen,
brandiger Schutt
die krustige Erde
decken,
über die Felder
von gestern
Vergessen gehen.

Todeszeichen
die Schatten
an den Ruinen.
Nie werden sie
zeugen müssen,
in ihrem

When the day
comes,
the day
of deathly silence,
bells will be muffled,
buds and flowers
will wither,
the stars will be
extinguished,
the tides
will stop flowing,
the air
will breathe
its last,
in fearful haste
our hands
will touch
in a last caress
before being consumed
by flaming sheaves.
Thus wedded,
we are born
to ashes.

————

The smoke
will be blown away,
burnt debris
covering
the charred earth,
it will pass over
the forgotten fields of yesterday.

The shadows
on the ruins
are signs of death.
In their numbness
they will never
bear witness
nor serve anyone again.

Erstarren,
niemandem mehr
werden sie dienen.

Kein Gott und Messias
wird niedersteigen,
um neue Geschlechter
zu küren,
des Donners Echo
in die Unendlichkeit
ein letztes
menschliches Seufzen
entführen.

No God or Messiah
will come down
to save
new races.
The echo of thunder
in infinity
will muffle
the last human sigh.

Der Patient

Als der Teufel im Sterben lag.
drängten die Ärzte an sein Krankenbett.
Sie untersuchten ihn vorn und untersuchten ihn hinten,
auskultierten ihn und maßen seinen Blutdruck
und wollten ihm das überflüssige Organ seines Schweifes
chirurgisch entfernen
Da zitterte der Teufel und bat mit leiser Stimme:
Laßt mir den Schweif, dann mach ich euch zu meinen Erben.
Man gab ihm vielerlei Medikamente
und injizierte ihm Dipsohydrol.
Ein Weißbekittelter flüsterte zum andern:
Herr Kollega, *ut aliquid fieri videatur* . . .
Der andere Weißbekittelte flüsterte:
Medicis praesentibus diabolus non moritur.
Da lachte der Teufel in sich hinein
und begann zu genesen.

MICHAEL GUTTENBRUNNER

(1919–   )

Born in Althofen, Michael Guttenbrunner as a young man was employed for a time as a groom
and as a construction worker. He was imprisoned by the Gestapo in 1938, then was enlisted into
the army, where he was wounded, court-martialed, and condemned to death. Somehow he
managed to survive the war. He found a position in the cultural section of the Carinthian
government in 1947.

Since that year Guttenbrunner has also been recognized as a distinguished poet, a poet whose
concerns are for suffering and political violence but who demonstrates the control and distance
and linguistic skill of a Karl Kraus and sometimes the melancholy of a Georg Trakl. Guttenbrun-
ner (under the pseudonym of "Strassbourg") once wrote a surrealistic play for Max Hölzer's
Surrealistische Publikationen, but his roots are in the working class, and his verse is often dialect
verse, following in this respect the lead of Theodor Kramer. Guttenbrunner's poems are collected
in several books, beginning with *Schwarze Ruten* [Black branches] of 1947, most recently in *Der
Abstieg* [The descent] of 1975 and *Gesang der Schiffe* [Song of the ships] of 1980. Guttenbrunner
is a member of the Austrian P.E.N. Club.

The Patient

As the devil lay dying
doctors crowded around his sickbed.
The examined him outside and in,
they took his pulse and his blood pressure
and wanted to amputate that superfluous organ,
his tail.
Having heard, the devil trembled and pleaded:
Let my tail be, and I'll make you my heirs.
They stuffed him with drugs
and gave him a Dipsohydrol injection.
One white-clad man whispered to the other:
Ut aliquid fieri videatur . . . *
The other white-clad man whispered:
Medicis praesentibus diabolus non moritur.**
At that the devil laughed up his sleeve
and began to recover.

**In order to do something it must be seen.*
***In the presence of doctors the Devil himself is not to die.*

Val d'Annivier

Ein langer, schwanker Ast
über den Abgrund gebreitet
mit hängenden Dörfern
gedrängt
wie mit Früchten belastet.
Wie Trauben, grünumschattet,
hängen über:
Chandolin, Vissoie, St. Luc,
St. Jean, Grimentz, Ayer
in hoher Luft, kochend im Licht.

Heimkehr

Ein Wandrer nähert sich
auf fast verwachsnem Pfad
dem Heimatdorf,
den wunderlichen Formen
seiner Verkommenheit.
Er möchte schreiend
an Tür und Fenster stürzen,
kniet aber nun
noch einen Steinwurf weit
und weint.

Hitler und die Generale

Er war schlecht und verdarb alles;
sie waren gut;
sooft er das Schwert schändete und stumpfte:
sie reichten es ihm neugeschärft wieder,
drückten es ihm immer wieder in die Hand.

Der Abstieg

Unter dir
immer wieder
ein tiefer stehender
Wirbel; nie ein Fuß.

Val d'Annivier

A long swaying branch
spread above the chasm
dense
with hanging villages
as if weighed down by fruit.
Like grapes in green foliage,
they hang there:
Chandolin, Vissoie, St. Luc,
St. Jean, Grimentz, Ayer,
high up, seething in light.

Homecoming

A traveler approaches
his native village
on a tangled path,
seeing the strange imagery
of his own decay.
He wants to scream
and throw himself
against doors and windows
but kneels down,
a stone's throw away
and weeps.

Hitler and the Generals

He was evil and ruined everything;
they were good;
whenever he dishonored and dulled the sword,
they presented it newly sharpened
and handed it to him again and again.

The Descent

Under you
again and again
ever more deeply established
chaos; there's never a foothold.

Ich habe
die Nacht
in
kleine schwarze
Würfel zerteilt

Das Kind
meines Nachbarn
spielt
mit diesen
dunklen Steinen

Es wirft sie
in den Fluß
und baut schwarze
Pyramiden

Ich gehe
pausenlos
durch
den
Tag

Doch
die Sonne

WALTHER NOWOTNY

(1 9 2 4 –   )

An actor and director on Austrian state radio (ORF), Walther Nowotny has lived since 1950 in Klagenfurt, where he has been a leading figure in theater and cultural activities. He has published poetry, prose, essays, dramatic reviews, and is the author of dramas and radio plays. His poems have appeared in *Eisenrose* [Iron rose] and *Bewegungen* [Movements] with those of other Austrian poets, and his own first collection, *Ich kann nur gegen die Wölfe schreiben* [I can only write against the wolves], was published in Rumania in 1981. His most recent collection, *Vor mir Stand die Zeit* [Time stood before me], appeared in 1984.

Nowotny is a founder and organizer of the annual International Literary Symposium in Fresach, Carinthia, president of the Carinthian Writers Association, and a member of the Austrian P.E.N. Club.

———

I've divided
the night
into small black dice

My neighbor's son
plays with
these dark stones

He throws them
into the river
and builds
black pyramids

I continually
walk through
the day

But the sun
does not replace
my lost nights

Yesterday
I secretly
retrieved
two small

ersetzt mir
meine verschenkten
Nächte
nicht

Gestern
habe ich
heimlich
zwei
kleine schwarze
Würfel
aus dem Fluß
geholt

Ich möchte
so gerne
die Sterne
wiedersehen.

————

Auf dem Blatt
meiner Uhr
rasen sinnlos
die Zeiger
Das Atom
hat
die Stunde
gelöscht
doch
auf der
flachen Hand
parkt
keine Sekunde.

————

Die Bilanz
eines
Tages
hat den
blutigen
Saum
eines
Schlachthofes

black dice
from the river

I would
so like
to see
the stars
once more.

———

The hands
on the dial
of my watch
spin senselessly.
The hours
have been
extinguished
by the atom
yet
not one second
lingers
on the palm
of my hand.

———

The balance sheet
of a day
has the
bloodstained
hem
of the
slaughterhouse

Der Mensch
tritt
als
Unmensch
in deinen
Schlaf

Die Wahrheit
des Weines
verstummt

Die
uniformierte
Lüge
zieht ein
Nachthemd an

Kotze kräftig
in den
Ausguß

Wirf
die Tageszeitung
nach
und
gib dir selber
eine
Chance.

―――――

Der Traumhund
ist von der Kette
Im Schaukelstuhl
der Tage
kläfft er
die Minuten
Das noch immer
nachtschwarze
Fell
dunkelt
so manchen
Tag
Seine

Man
enters
your sleep
like
a monster

The truth
of wine
makes us mute

The
uniformed
lie
dons a
nightshirt

Puke vigorously
in the
sink

Throw
today's paper
in the same place
and
give yourself
a chance.

———

The dreamdog
has broken his chain
He barks
at the minutes
in the rocking chair
of days
His coat
still black
as night
darkens
some days
His red tongue
hangs out of

rote Zunge
überlappt
das Gebiß
Vielleicht
werden wir
Sonnenwandler
endlich
erwachen
wenn
der
Traumhund
uns beißt.

his mouth
Perhaps
we day-walkers
will
finally
awake
when
the dreamdog
bites us.

———————

Reisen wir

Aber wohin
frage ich

Heimwärts

Aber wo ist das
frage ich

Innen
sagte die Stimme

———————

Daß deine Schlinge
mit der du mich einfingst
aus Gold ist
was hilft mirs
immer fester ziehst du sie zu

Ziehe nur zu
Immer leiser
lerne ich atmen
immer leichter
die Füße heben
(wenn du mich schleuderst)
weg von der Erde

DORIS MÜHRINGER

(1920 –   )

Born in Graz, Doris Mühringer now lives and writes—both for children and for adults—in Vienna. Her poems (very much for adults) have been collected in several books, all entitled simply *Gedichte; Gedichte I* appeared in 1957, *Gedichte II* in 1969, *Gedichte III* in 1972. Mühringer is a member of the Austrian P.E.N. Club.

———

Let's travel

where to
I ask

home

but where is that
I ask

within
the voice replied

———

What good does the fact
that the loop
with which you have caught me
is made of gold
do me
you keep tightening it

Pull it tighter now
I learn to breathe
ever more softly
and to lift my feet
ever more lightly
(when you fling me)
from this earth

Als ich ein Kind war
und lernte gehn
und ging
und ging in die Schule
und ging
und ging in die Schule des Lebens
wie man so sagt
und niemals mehr sollt ich im Park
spielen
oder in andren Gespinsten—
Da ging ich abends hinaus
es war Vollmond:
aufs Fensterbrett in der Stadt
und ging voll Mond
und ging
und ging um
ging um und umging
auf diese Weise
wie man so sagt
die Schule des Lebens

Immer wieder

Anfangen
lasset uns anfangen
lasset uns alles neu anfangen
So fingen sie an
und fingens so an

Einfangen
laßt sie uns einfangen
laßt sie uns alle einfangen
Los
fangt sie ein
fangt sie ab
fangt sie
fangt sie
f a n g t !
Und ab und ans Kreuz mit ihnen

Anfangen
lasset uns anfangen

———

When I was a child
and learned to walk
and walked
and went to school
and went
and went to the school of life
as they say
and I could no longer
play in the park
nor in other fanciful places
One evening
in the city
when the moon was full
I climbed out onto the window ledge
filled with moon
and walked
and walked out
and walked out and avoided
in this way
what they call
the school of life

Again and Again

Begin
let's begin
let's all begin again
So they began
and that's how they began

Get 'em
let's get 'em
let's get 'em all
Now
let's get 'em
let's catch 'em
get 'em
get 'em
Go!
Nail 'em to the cross

Begin
let's begin

lasset uns alles neu anfangen
So fingen sie an
und fingens so an

Einfangen
laßt sie uns einfangen
laßt sie uns alle einfangen
Los
Fangt sie ein
fangt sie ab
fangt sie
fangt sie
f a n g t !
Und ab und ans Kreuz mit ihnen

Anfangen (da capo)

let's begin again
So they began
and that's how they began

Get 'em
let's get 'em
let's get 'em all
Now
let's get 'em
catch 'em
get 'em
get 'em
Go!
Nail 'em to the cross

Begin (*da capo*)

The Postwar Generation

Reklame

Wohin aber gehen wir
ohne sorge sei ohne sorge
wenn es dunkel und wenn es kalt wird
sei ohne sorge
aber
mit musik
was sollen wir tun
heiter und mit musik
und denken
heiter
angesichts eines Endes
mit musik
und wohin tragen wir
am besten
unsre Fragen und den Schauer aller Jahre
in die Traumwäscherei ohne sorge sei ohne sorge
was aber geschieht

INGEBORG BACHMANN

(1926–1973)

One of the finest writers in German to appear since the war, Ingeborg Bachmann was born in Klagenfurt in 1926. She studied philosophy (particularly Heidegger and existentialism) at the University of Vienna and first undertook an academic career. She lived in Paris from 1951 to 1953 and later in New York and in Frankfurt, where she taught poetry at the university. In 1973 she was burned to death in her apartment in Rome.

Bachmann's first notable appearance as a poet was at a reading before "Gruppe 47," a collective of German-language writers, in 1952; her best known poem, "Grosse Landschaft bei Wien," established her reputation. Bachmann is known as a difficult, highly literate, and philosophical poet in the mainstream of poetry in German, the tradition of Hölderlin and Rilke. She was also a passionate yet contemplative writer who gained perspective on her intensity by complex allusions which ranged widely over the literatures of the West. Her poems appeared in two collections, *Die gestundete Zeit* [Delayed time] (1953) and *Anrufung des Grossen Bären* [Calling the great bear] (1956).

Ingeborg Bachmann was also a distinguished prose writer. Her radio plays—notably *Der gute Gott von Manhattan* [God in Manhattan] (1958)—her distinguished novel *Malina* (1971), and her stories—*Das Dreißigste Jahr* [The thirtieth year] (1961, 1966) and *Simultan* (1972)—show the main direction she took in the later years of her career. Ingeborg Bachmann's collected works (*Werke*) were published in four volumes in 1978.

Advertising

Where are we going
don't worry don't worry
when it gets dark and cold
don't worry
but
with music
what shall we do
cheerfully and with music
and think
cheerfully
in view of an ending
with music
and where should we take
in the best way
our questions and the horror of all our years
to the dream laundry don't worry don't worry
but what will happen

am besten
wenn Totenstille

eintritt

Nach dieser Sintflut

Nach dieser Sintflut
möchte ich die Taube,
und nichts als die Taube,
noch einmal gerettet sehn.

Ich ginge ja unter in diesem Meer!
flög' sie nicht aus,
brächte sie nicht
in letzter Stunde das Blatt.

Hôtel de la Paix

Die Rosenlast stürzt lautlos von den Wänden,
und durch den Teppich scheinen Grund und Boden.
Das Lichtherz bricht der Lampe.
Dunkel. Schritte.
Der Riegel hat sich vor den Tod geschoben.

Exil

Ein Toter bin ich der wandelt
gemeldet nirgends mehr
unbekannt im Reich des Präfekten
überzählig in den goldenen Städten
und im grünenden Land

abgetan lange schon
und mit nichts bedacht

Nur mit Wind mit Zeit und mit Klang

der ich unter Menschen nicht leben kann

Ich mit der deutschen Sprache
dieser Wolke um mich

all's for the best
when deathly silence

enters

After This Flood

After this flood
I'd like to see the dove,
and only the dove,
saved once more.

I would have drowned in that sea
if it hadn't flown off
and brought
the bough at the last moment.

Hôtel de la Paix

Silently the walls shed their burden of roses
The floor, the ground, shine through the carpet
The lamp's heart of light is shattered.
Darkness. Steps.
The bolt has been thrown against Death.

Exile

I'm one of the wandering dead
no longer registered anywhere
unknown in the realm of the prefect
superfluous in the golden cities
and in the greening countryside

disposed of long ago
and endowed with nothing

Only with wind with time and with sound

I who cannot live among people

With the German language
with this cloud about me

die ich halte als Haus
treibe durch alle Sprachen

O wie sie sich verfinstert
die dunklen die Regentöne
nur die wenigen fallen

In hellere Zonen trägt dann sie den Toten hinauf

Enigma
Für Hans Werner Henze aus der Zeit der Ariosi

Nichts mehr wird kommen.

Frühling wird nicht mehr werden.
Tausendjährige Kalender sagen es jedem voraus.

Aber auch Sommer und weiterhin, was so gute Namen
wie «sommerlich" hat—
es wird nichts mehr kommen.

Du sollst ja nicht weinen,
sagt eine Musik.

Sonst
sagt
niemand
etwas.

that I keep as a home
I move through all languages

O how it grows dark
the gloomy tones of rain
only a little falls

The cloud then lifts the dead to brighter regions

Enigma
For Hans Werner Henze at the time of Ariosi*

Nothing more will come

It will never be spring again.
Thousand-year almanacs predict it for everyone.

Nor summer, nor anything so pleasantly referred to
as "summery"—
nothing more will come.

You mustn't cry
says the music.

Other than that
no one
says
anything.

*In 1952 Bachmann collaborated with the composer Hans Werner Henze in a ballet version of
Dostoyevsky's* The Idiot *and in 1960 in an operatic version of Kleist's* Der Prinz von Homburg.
Henze later (1963) composed Ariosi [Arias], *based on a lyric sequence by Torquato Tasso.*

Der Knabe

An einer trockenen Bananenschale
hing noch ein Stück verdorrte Frucht
und der Geruch von einer fernen, warmen Bucht.

Er roch daran zum ersten Male
und wurde gleich der Diener einer Sucht
und schnitt aus Schulpapier ein Schiff zu seiner Flucht.

———————

Der Himmel wurde gelb wie schäbiges Papier.
Die staubige Allee verkam vor Langeweile.
Sie schrieb die immer gleiche, krumme Zeile
verbogner «i» mit ungenauer Hand
ins braun und lila Herbstzeitlosenland.
Ein Wasserfarbenmond war wie ein Fleck auf schäbigem Papier.

HERTHA KRÄFTNER

(1928 – 1951)

The daughter of a radical socialist political organizer, Hertha Kräftner was born in Rosenau, in Sonntagberg, in 1928 and lived in Mattersburg until the death of her father at the hands of the occupying Russians in 1945. She then went to Vienna, where she studied German and English literature at the university. There she fell in love with a young man (her "Anatol") and in 1948 published her first poem. Kräftner concluded her studies in 1950 (with a thesis on surrealism in Franz Kafka) and was soon on her way to being established as one of the important young Viennese writers, with poems in *Neue Wege* and with readings on Radio Wien and in Salzburg. But she experienced recurring depressions of increasing frequency and duration, and on November 11, 1951, Hertha Kräftner took her own life by drinking Veronal.

Kräftner's work appeared in various journals and collections of the 1950s, including *Neue Wege*, *Die Zeit*, and Andreas Okopenko's *Publikationen Einer Wiener Gruppe Junger Autoren* [Publications of a group of young Viennese writers], but her work was not collected until 1963, when her poems and her remarkable diary were edited by Okopenko and Otto Breicha and published by Stiasny Verlag, Graz. This collection, *Das Werk,* was republished in 1977 by Edition Roetzer and thus reached a greater audience. And another collection, *Das blaue Licht* [The blue light], also edited by Breicha and Okopenko, appeared from Luchterhand in 1981.

The Boy

In a withered banana peel
there was still a rotting piece of the fruit
and the smell of a warm and distant bay.

Smelling it for the first time
he was caught up in his desire
and made a ship out of notebook paper to sail away.

———

The sky turned as yellow as cheap paper.
The dust-covered lane yawned and died.
She kept on writing the letter "i"
crookedly with an unsteady hand
in a brown and lilac autumn crocus land.
A water-colored moon was like a spot on cheap paper.

Litanei

Du steinerner Engel über dem Leid.
Nächtlicher Vogel mit traurigem Flügelschlag.
Mondland in Gelb und Grau.
Blässe von Aaronstab.
Lilafarbenes Blatt einer Schwertlilie.
Wildes Geschrei des Zigeuners mit trockenem Blut an den Händen.
Schale voll Nesseln und blühendem Gras.
Klagendes Lied von bettelnden Kindern.
Stöhnender Tod einer wahnsinnigen Frau.
Flüsternde Demut weißrindiger Birken.
Sanftes Gekräusel des Baches um rundgewaschene Steine . . .
Bist du das alles oder das Bild einer Liebe?
Ich tat mein Herz auf für dich,
und die Welt kam verworren herein.

Die Frau des Henkers

Die Frau des Henkers aß eines Mittags nicht mehr weiter.
Ihr Mann verspeiste grad ein junges Huhn.
Sie sah ihm zu . . . und waßte nicht,
warum sie sich an ihren Hochzeitstag erinnern mußte
und an die Myrthen, und daß jemand sang.
Es war ein weißes Huhn gewesen,
so sanft und weiß und warm
und ganz geduldig unter dem Messer.
Nun aß es ihr Mann, und ein Tropfen Fett
rann über seine weiß gebürsteten Finger.

Da schrie sie, ganz so, wie ihr Mann
es von manchen Verurteilten erzählte,
wenn sie ihn sahen.
Sie schrie und stieß ihren Teller von sich
und lief hinaus, durch den kleinen Vorgarten
und die Straßen der Stadt,
durch das Feld mit Mohn
und das Feld mit Weizen
und das Feld mit dem grünen Klee.
Sie suchten sie lange vergeblich.

Litany

Stone angel looking down on suffering.
Night-bird with wings beating sadly.
Moonscape in yellow and gray.
Pallor of Aaron's rod.
Lilac-colored leaf of an iris.
Wild cries of the gipsy with dried blood on his hands.
Cup full of nettles and fresh grass.
Plaintive song of beggar children.
Moaning death of a mad woman.
Whispering humility of a white-ringed birch.
Soft ruffling of a brook rounding smooth stones . . .
Are you all that or an image of love?
I opened my heart to you,
and the world stumbled in.

The Hangman's Wife

Once, at midday, the hangman's wife stopped eating.
Her husband was eating a young hen.
She watched him . . . and didn't know why
she was reminded of her wedding day,
and of the myrtle, and that someone had sung.
It had been a white hen,
so tender and white and warm
and very patient under the knife.
Now her husband was eating it, and a drop of fat
ran over his manicured white fingers.

Her screams were like the condemned
when they caught sight of her husband
according to his descriptions.
She screamed and pushed her plate away
and ran out through the small front garden
and through the streets of the city,
through the field of poppies
and the field of wheat
and the field with green clover.
For a long time they searched,
but they never found her.

Mit frühen Weidenkätzchen

Es war ein Himmel von Türkis,
der sich der Stadt nur zögernd überließ.
Aber ein Teich war hinterm Häuserrand,
der in der braunen Wiese lag
wie eine glatte Hand;
in ihm verhieß
der Himmel seinen neuen Tag.
Und eine unsichtbare Flöte
verharrte lang in einem Ton wie im Gebete.

With Early Cattails

Reluctantly a turquoise sky
surrendered itself to the town.
But there was a pond in a brown field
behind a row of houses;
it bore the sky's promise
of a new day
like an outstretched palm.
An invisible flute
held a long note like a prayer.

———————

mi kennans ned
debbad mochn
i bi scho
fufzg joa
bei da baddei

i bi scho
med mein faddan
aum ring
midmaschiad
untan kaisa
franz josef
mi kennans ned
debbad mochn

JOSEF MAYER-LIMBERG

(1 9 1 1 –   )

Born in Limberg in Upper Austria, Josef Mayer moved to Vienna in 1929 and made the capital his city. He studied history, art history, and German literature at the University of Vienna, but his studies were interrupted by the war. He was conscripted into the Wehrmacht and served on the Russian front, and later in Italy.

After the war he returned to Vienna, and his poems from *Einfahrt* [Entry], which had been praised by its editor at Albert-Verlag in 1940 but not published then because of the wartime paper shortages, began to appear in literary journals and newspapers. In 1956 Mayer-Limberg settled in Ottakring, a working-class district of Vienna. He was a frequenter of the coffeehouses and cafés of his district in the early 1960s, and it was then that he became interested in its dialect and in the tradition of dialect poetry, established in the 1930s by Josef Weinheber and revitalized in the late 1950s by H. C. Artmann.

Mayer-Limberg's own dialect poems were not published until 1973, in *fon de möada und de hausmasda: gedichda aus oddagring* [about murderers and superintendents: poems from ottakring]. Mayer-Limberg's most recent collection is *eilodung zu de hausmasda: neucha gedichda aus oddagring* [invitation to the superintendents: new poems from ottakring] (1978). Josef Mayer-Limberg is a member of the Austrian P.E.N. Club.

Although chronologically he is older than the other poets in this section, Josef Mayer-Limberg's recent appearance on the literary scene and his intensely contemporary subject matter and language place him, not among Austria's "Older Generation" of contemporary poets, nor even among those whose orientation and subject matter identify them as "The Generation of the War," but rather in the generation which, if one considers patterns of influence, is to be seen as the successor of Artmann. Accordingly we have placed Mayer-Limberg among "The Postwar Poets."

I'm nobody's fool
I've been in the party
for half a century

in the days
of franz josef
I marched
on the ring
with my red flag
holding daddy's hand
I'm nobody's fool

da koal max
is ma wuaschd
den faschdee i ned
de baddei
wiad scho wissn
woss duad

und wauns a
an offn aufschdön
so wöli eam a
de baddei
wiad scho wissn
woss duad

i bi scho
fufzg joa
bei da baddei
mi kennans ned
debbad mochn

ösdareicha

noch 18

soziobussla
pfoarafressa

noch 34

sozifressa
pfoaraobussla

noch 38

naziobussla
 judnfressa

noch 45

judnobussla
nazifressa

I don't know
much about marx
crime stories
are more my style
but so what
the party's my guide

and if they tell me
to vote for a baboon
that's what I'll do
the party's my guide

I've been in the party
half a century
I'm nobody's fool

austrians

after 18

redlovers
priestloathers

after 34

redloathers
priestlovers

after 38

nazilovers
jewloathers

after 45

jewlovers
naziloathers

noch 55

ewech neutral
ewech
a schdingada kas

————

bluman
bluman
bluman

owa
deataumbombm

bluman
bluman und
beadde

owa
de ataumbombm

bluman
bluman
beadde und
haschisch

owa
de ataumbombm

bluman
bluman
beadde
haschisch und
noggade

owa
de ataumbombm

de ataumbombm
deara is des
wuaschd

after 55

eternally neutral
eternally
a smelly cheese

———

flowers
flowers
flowers

but
the bomb

flowers
flowers and
beards

but
the bomb

flowers
flowers
beards and
hash

but
the bomb

flowers
flowers
beards
hash and
nudes

but
the bomb

the bomb
it's all
the same
the bomb

de schded
foan baradis
wia de engl
med de
feirechn schweadda

do kumd
kana mea
eine

des besde
wos eana
bassian kau
is

so kuman
noch gugging
und mochn
gedichda
fian
navratil

———————

a aggd
zwa aggdn
fia aggdn

dausnd
dausnd
aggdn

enda
gaunzn
gaunzn wöd

a hofrod
zwa hofred
fia hofred

it stands
before paradise gate
like the angel
with the fiery sword

no one can
get by

the only thing
that you can do
about it

is to go
to the nuthouse
and write
poems
for navratil*

————

one file
two files
four files

thousands
and thousands
of files

in the
whole
wide
world

one civil servant
two civil servants
four civil servants

*Dr. Leo Navratil, an Austrian psychiatrist, has published several collections of poems by inmates of mental institutions.

dausnd
dausnd
hofred

enda
gaunzn
gaunzn
wöd

a unddaschrifd
zwa unddaschrifdn
fia unddaschrifdn

dausnd
dausnd
unddaschrifdn

fon de
dausnd
dausnd
hofred

auf de
dausnd
dausnd
aggdn

enda
gaunzn
gaunzn
wöd

a glana
zwa glane
fia glane

dausnd
dausnd
glane
fliangschiss

auf de
dausnd
dausnd
aggdn

thousands
and thousands
of civil servants

in the
whole
wide
world

one signature
two signatures
four signatures

thousands
and thousands
of signatures

of thousands
and thousands
of civil servants

on thousands
and thousands
of files

in the
whole
wide
world

one little
two little
four little

thousands
and thousands
of fly specks

on the
thousands
and thousands
of files

med de
dausnd
dausnd
unddaschrifdn

fon de
dausnd
dausnd
hofred

enda
gaunzn
gaunzn
wöd

———

da lenin
woa en wean

da schdalin
woa en wean

da hiddla
woa en wean

da gruschdschof
woa en wean

da kenedi
woa en wean

de essess
woa en wean

de russn
woan en wean

es muas do wos
drau sei aun uns

nua da gödde
hod net heagfundn

with the
thousands
and thousands
of signatures

of the
thousands
and thousands
of civil servants

in the
whole
wide
world

————

lenin
came to vienna

stalin
came to vienna

hitler
came to vienna

khruschchev
came to vienna

kennedy
came to vienna

the ss
came to vienna

the russians
came to vienna

we must have
something

only goethe
didn't come here

dea buaschoa
und dinsdmalfafiara

des is
dübbesch

that bourgeois
that seducer of servant girls

that's
typical

Früheres Bild

Saß ich wo auf warmen weißen Stufen,
Saß ich wo und wurde braungeschienen,
Kam ein Käfer aus dem Busch gefahren.

Hörte einen lieben Namen rufen,
Sah den Rufen nach und zog mit ihnen
Irgendhin.—Das war mit vierzehn Jahren.

Im August

In den Viadukten der Stadt
liegt der Geruch der Märkte.
Er sitzt zu Mittag auf dem Asphalt
und frischt einmal angenehm auf,
wenn gegen sechzehn Uhr Wind kommt.

Er bleibt den nächsten Tag
und den übernächsten so stark.

ANDREAS OKOPENKO

(1930 –)

Andreas Okopenko was born in Košice (Kaschau), Czechoslovakia, in 1930. Trained as a chemist, he settled in Vienna and in the 1950s began to publish his poetry. Very soon he was the central figure in a circle of antiestablishment writers who were to become the Vienna Group. Okopenko's *Grüner November* [Green November] appeared in 1957 and *Seltsame Tage* [Strange days] in 1963. In 1969 *Warum sind die Latrinen so traurig? Spleengesang* [Why are latrines so sad? Spleen-song] made his popular reputation.

Okopenko has since written an experimental novel, *Lexikon einer sentimentalen Reise zum Exporteurtreffen in Druden* [Dictionary of a sentimental journey to a meeting of export officers in Druden] (1970), in which he provides the reader with a new alphabet for him to arrange. In *Der Akazienfresser* [The acacia eater] (1973) Okopenko proposes a new punctuation mark to indicate boredom. In 1974 he published a play and a collection of his fantastic stories, *Warnung für Ypsilon* [Warning for Upsilon], which was very well received. In 1976 another novel, *Meteoriten* [Meteorites], appeared, and it was followed in 1977 by *Vier Aufsätze* [Four compositions]. In 1980 his *Gesammelte Lyrik* [Collected poems] was published.

Okopenko is a founding member of the Graz Authors' Collective.

Early Impression

Somewhere I sat on warm white steps
Somewhere I sat tanning in the sun
And watched an insect come out of the bushes.

I heard someone call a beloved name
And went in the direction of the call.
Somewhere—that was at age fourteen.

August

The odor of the market
lies in the viaducts of the city.
At noon it sits on the asphalt
and is made fresh again
by the four o'clock wind

It lingers the following day
as well as the day after that.

Er weiß um den Herbst,
der nach ihm kommt.
Der mit Azetylen und Teer
in die Viadukte zieht
und mit dünnem Rauch aufsteigt
in die einsamen Himmel
der Menschen.

Im August
2

Die nicht enden will Landschaft
Wolken aus Blaugrau und Ziegelrot
vor dem grünen Himmel,
in den grün-violett die Straßenbahnen blitzen.

Abend trägt ferne Musik herüber
Abend raschelt in den Bäumen,

Nur Wind entlang der Leitung
surrt metallisch fremd
eine Weile in den grünen Himmel.

Garten

Der tiefe Garten
dunkelgrüner Blätter,
die vom Boden kommen
und feucht sind.

Braune Erde,
unter dem Blattwerk
wach.

Garten . . .
Drinnen
ein Weg,
unter hohem Gras.

Der Morgen
jung und rauchblau:
hier drüber
beginnt er.

It knows the coming
of autumn
and enters the viaducts
with acetylene and tar
and ascends in thin smoke
to the lonely heaven
of man.

August
2

The landscape that doesn't want to end,
blue-gray and brick-red clouds
in a green sky,
reflected in the green-violet streetcars.

Evening carries the sound of distant music,
Evening rustles in the trees.

Only the wind along electrical wires
purrs metallically strange
for a while in the green sky.

Garden

Deep garden
of dark-green leaves
they come from the ground
and are moist.

Brown earth
awakes
under the leaves.

Garden . . .
inside
a path
under high grass.

The morning
young and smoke-blue
begins
here.

Vor Mittag
scheint die Sonne
halb herein.

Oh, der Tag
ist hier
lang
bis zum Abend.

Und dann
naht das andere Grün
langsam
die Nacht.

Garten:
Von den Schatten
atmet es
warm. . . .

Before noon
the sun
half shines here.

O day
is here
a long time,
up until evening.

And then
green darkens
slowly
into night.

Garden:
breathing in
the warmth
of the shadows. . . .

ich bin ein wirkliches kind

ich bin ein wirkliches kind
nein nein so etwas
ja so etwas
ein wirkliches kind
nein nein so etwas
wirklich ein kind
so ein kind
nein nein so etwas
wirklich ein kind
bin ich
nein nein so etwas
bin ich wirklich ein kind?
nein nein
ein wirkliches kind
nein ein kind?
wirklich nein so etwas
ein kind

niemand hilft mir

niemand hilft mir
niemand spricht mir

KONRAD BAYER

(1932 – 1964)

Born in Vienna in 1932, Konrad Bayer had a considerably varied career—as a musician, bank employee, and actor—before his association with the Vienna Group and his real commitment to a career as a writer in the late 1950s. He worked as an actor in literary cabaret in 1958, and by 1959 he had risen to a position of eminence in the Group—so much so that after his suicide in 1964 the Group ceased to meet.

A film scenarist as well as a poet, Bayer developed the dadaist tradition experimentally in the direction of "concrete" poetry. For a time he was (perhaps, with Mayröcker) one of the more theoretically committed practitioners of *Konkretismus* among the Vienna poets of the 1960s. Bayer shared with Artmann and other members of the Group a sheer delight in language and in words as individual acts of imagination.

Konrad Bayer's collected work (*Die Gesamtwerke*) was published in 1977 by Rowohlt Verlag, edited by Gerhard Rühm.

i'm a true child

i'm a true child
no no really
that's too much
a true child
no no really
truly a child
that kind of a child
no really
truly a child
i am
no no really
am i truly a child?
no no
a true child
no a child?
no really truly
a child

nobody helps me

nobody helps me
nobody speaks to me

niemand gibt mir ein stück brot
jeder betrachtet mich
jeder verachtet mich
jeder wünscht ich wäre tot
das ist lustig
das ist schön
das ist das zugrundegehn

niemand weint so zart
wie es meine art
niemand wälzt sich so im kot
jeder ist entsetzt
jeder ist verletzt
jeder flüstert leis «mein gott"
das ist lustig
das ist schön
das ist das zugrundegehn

ich und mein körper

ich und mein körper wollen verreisen
ich und mein körper
mein körper und ich
10 jahre später stehn wir am bahnsteig
ich und du mit unseren körpern
und wollen verreisen
du und dein körper
und ich und mein körper
stehen beisammen
und du steckst in deinem
körper und ich steck
in meinem körper

erstens will ich fröhlich sein

erstens will ich fröhlich sein
zweitens mich vergnügen
drittens ist die erde mein
das sollte doch genügen

aber ich
fürchterlich
hab auch noch das weltall

nobody gives me a piece of bread
everybody watches me
everybody puts me down
everybody wishes i were dead
that's amusing
that's beautiful
that's the end

nobody cries as softly
as i do
nobody rolls in shit this way
everybody is horrified
everybody is offended
everybody whispers "my god"
that's amusing
that's beautiful
that's the end

i and my body

i and my body want to take a trip
i and my body
my body and i
10 years later we stand on the station platform
i and you with our bodies
and want to take a trip
you and your body
and i and my body
stand next to each other
and you are stuck in your
body and i am stuck
in my body

first i want to be happy

first i want to be happy
second to enjoy myself
third the world is mine
that should be enough

but i
to my horror
also have the universe

und die zeit
und den raum
sowieso man glaubt es kaum

and time
and space
no one quite believes that anyway

die nacht
und die tochter der nacht
und die tochter der tochter der nacht
und die tochter der tochter der tochter der nacht

der tag
und der sohn des tages
und der sohn des sohnes des tages
und der sohn des sohnes des sohnes des tages

der sohn
und
die tochter

und alle ihre verwandten alle verwandten

sie blicken auf das geschwisterpaar

sie blicken auf den sohn und die tochter
des sohnes und der tochter

GERHARD RÜHM

(1 9 3 0 –   )

Born in Vienna, Gerhard Rühm was first known as one of the leaders of the Vienna Group, joining H. C. Artmann and Friedrich Achleitner in *Hosn rosn baa* of 1959, one of the Group's more important manifestations. Rühm was also to become the Vienna Group's historian, editing a retrospective anthology in 1967 (*Die Wiener Gruppe*).

Gerhard Rühm is, like many of his colleagues, a disciple of *Konkretismus,* and his poetry, published for the most part in eight collections in the 1960s, manifests that commitment. Rühm has also written several plays, and he was the collector and editor of the poems of his friend, Konrad Bayer. Gerhard Rühm's own collected poems and "visual texts" appeared in 1970 (*gesammlte gedichte und visuelle texte*) and continued to appear in later collections over the next decade.

In 1973 Rühm was a founding member of the Graz Authors' Collective. He is also one of the leaders of the attack—both in public manifestations and in published poetry—on the traditions of bourgeois propriety and manners, and on the values on which they are based, both of which are still clearly manifest in Austrian life today.

Rühm has served as a professor of music at several German universities, and he is also recognized as a visual artist.

---

the night
and the daughter of the night
and the daughter of the daughter of the night
and the daughter of the daughter of the daughter of the night

the day
and the son of the day
and the son of the son of the day
and the son of the son of the son of the day

the son
and
the daughter

and all their relatives all relatives

they look at the brother and sister

they look at the son and the daughter
of the son and of the daughter

des sohnes und der tochter
des sohnes und der tochter

und es wird tag
und es wird nacht

gib mir die hand

gib mir die hand luise
deine kalte hand

gib mir die hand luise
die kalte hand

nicht beide hände luise
nicht beide

nur eine hand luise gib
eine kalte hand

ich drücke sie nicht
ich halte sie nur

ich will sie nicht drücken
nur halten

deine hand luise
deine hand

deine kalte hand die kalte hand
halte ich nur

ein blick in deine kühlen augen
genügt dabei

ein blick in deine kühlen augen
genügt

zwei blicke wären schon zu viel
viel zu viel

zwei blicke wären zu viel
einer genügt

of the son and of the daughter
of the son and of the daughter

and day comes
and night comes

give me your hand

give me your hand louise
your cold hand

give me your hand louise
your cold hand

not both hands louise
not both

only one hand louise give
one cold hand

i won't squeeze it
i'll only hold it

i don't want to squeeze it
only hold it

your hand louise
your hand

your cold hand the cold hand
i only hold

one glance into your cool eyes
is enough

one glance into your cool eyes
is enough

two glances would be too much
much too much

two glances would be too much
one is enough

leer
leer
leer
leer
leer
leer
leer
leer
leer
leer
leer
leer
leer
leer
leer
leer
leer
leer
leer
leer
leer
leer
leer
leer
leer
lärm lärm lärm lärm lärm lärm lärm   lärm lärm lärm lärm lärm lärm
leer
leer
leer
leer
leer
leer
leer
leer
leer
leer
leer
leer
leer
leer
leer
leer

———

empty
empty
empty
empty
empty
empty
empty
empty
empty
empty
empty
empty
empty
empty
empty
empty
empty
empty
empty
empty
empty
empty
empty
empty
empty
empty
empty

noise noise noise noise noise noise noise   noise noise noise noise noise noise

empty
empty
empty
empty
empty
empty
empty
empty
empty
empty
empty
empty
empty
empty
empty
empty

———

leib leib leib leib
leib leib leib leib
leib leib leib leib
leib leib leib leib
leib leib leib leib
leib leib leib leib
leib leib leibleib

blumenstück
für günter brus

die tulpe scheisst auf den rasen
das veilchen furzt in die hand des gärtners
das vergissmeinnicht kotzt ins seidenpapier
die nelke schlatzt auf den stengel
die orchidee onaniert zwischen den fingern des fräuleins
    und bekleckert sie bis in den ärmel hinein
die rose stinkt nach schweiss und menstruationsblut
das maiglöckchen rotzt auf das frische tischtuch
die lilie brunzt in die vase
die hyazinthe rülpst auf

body body body body
body body body body
body body body body
body body body body
body body body body
body body body body
body body bodybody

flower play
for günter brus

the tulip shits on the lawn
the violet farts in the gardener's hand
the forget-me-not pukes in the tissue paper
the carnation spits on its stem
the orchid jerks off between the girl's fingers
     and befouls her way up inside her sleeve
the rose stinks of sweat and menstrual blood
the lily-of-the-valley snots on the fresh tablecloth
the lily pisses in the vase
the hyacinth belches

FRIEDRICH ACHLEITNER

(1930–)

A member of the Vienna Group, Friedrich Achleitner began his career as a visual artist and architectural critic. For a period he divided his time between Vienna and Berlin. Today he is a professor of architecture in Vienna.

Achleitner's first collection of "texts" appeared in 1956, and *prosa, konstellationen, montagen, dialektgedichte, studien* [prose, constellations, montages, dialect poems, studies] appeared in 1970. In 1974 Rowohlt published *Quadratroman* [Square novel], and in 1975 *Quadratstudien* [Square studies] was published in Linz.

One of the most experimental of the concrete poets, Achleitner's poems are as visually committed as are Jandl's to sound experiment. The poems we have included here require no translation, as is immediately apparent.

———

a
so

so
a

m
hm

hm
hm

a
ha

so
so

———

bix
bum

fix

nix

————

biii bibibibibi
biii bibibibibi
biii bibibibibi

bilibilibilibili
bilibilibilibili
bilibilibilibili

biii bibibibibi
biii bibibibibi
biii bibibibibi

————

o o o o o o o o o o o o o o o o o o o o o
o o o o o o o o o o o o o o o o o o o o o
o o o o o o o o o o o o o o o o o o o o o
o o o o o o o o o o o o o o o o o o o o o
o o o o o o o o o o o o o o o o o o o o o
o o o o o o o o o o o o o o o o o o o o o
o o o o o o o o o o o o o o o o o o o o o
o o o o o o o o o o o o o o o o o o o o o
o o o o o o o o o o o o o o o o o o o o o
o o o o o o o o o o o o o o o o o o o o o
o o o o o o o o o o o o o o o o o o o o o
o o o o o o o o o o o o o o o o o o o o o
o o o o o o o o o o o o o o o o o o o o o
o o o o o o o o o o o o o o o o o o o o o
o o o o o o o o o o o o o o o o o o o o o
o o o o o o o o o o o o o o o o o o o o o
o o o o o o o o o o o o o o o o o o o o o
o o o o o o o o o o o o o o o o o o o o o
o o o o o o o o o o o o o o o o o o o o o
o o o o o o o o o o o o o o o o o o s o

lenin im winter

die revolution
die schneevolution
die teevolution
der schnee
der tee
der rehe

———————

leben
kleben

leben
kleben

ERNST JANDL

(1 9 2 5 –)

Perceived as one of Austria's more successful "concrete" poets when he was identified with the Vienna Group, Ernst Jandl today thinks of himself as a "sound" poet (of "Lautgedichte"). His public recitations are often marked by deliberate distortions of familiar words and other similar maneuvers. Also, although born and beginning his career as a teacher in Vienna, Jandl later associated himself with the activities of the Graz Group. He has lived in England, has written in English, and is today an active translator of contemporary English verse.

The wry humor which informs Jandl's convolute imagination is very much his own, although such humor is not atypical among the poets associated with the Vienna Group and the Graz Group. Beginning in 1956 with *Andere Augen* [Other eyes] Jandl has published well over a dozen collections of poems, at least one illustrated with his own drawings. *Laut und Luise* [Noise and Louise], certainly one of his more delightful collections, appeared in 1971, and *Serienfuss* [Foot in series], equally successful, was published in 1974. More recent is *die bearbeitung der mutze* [the care of a cap] of 1978 and *der gelbe hund* [the yellow dog] of 1980. A collection of Jandl's earlier poems in English translation, *No Music Please*, was published in 1967.

Ernst Jandl is also a playwright; he has collaborated with his close friend Friederike Mayröcker in the writing of several radio plays and has had significant success as a dramatic writer. Jandl's "speech opera," *Aus der Fremde* [From afar] appeared in print in 1980. Now the vice-president of the Graz Authors' Collective, Jandl has firmly established himself as the opponent of all conservative tendencies in the arts.

lenin in winter

the revolution
the rearvolution
the bearvolution
the rear
the bear
the deer

———

to live
to glue

to live
to glue

die dinge
mit augen

die dinge
mit augen

die dinge
mit augen
bekleben

sehen
sehen
sehen

einst und jetzt

einst keiner
jetzt einer

einst und jetzt

einst einer
jetzt einer

einst und jetzt

einst einer
jetzt keiner

einst und jetzt

abschied

unsermund
unsere hände
adieu
    adieu

———

und weinte bitterlich
und doktor oppelt kam
und weinte bitterlich

things
with eyes

things
with eyes

to glue
things
to eyes

to see
to see
to see

once and now

once no one
now someone

once and now

once someone
now someone

once and now

once someone
now no one

once and now

parting

ourmouth
our hands
adieu
    adieu

———

and cried bitterly
and doctor oppelt came
and cried bitterly

und frau direktor reichert kam
und weinte bitterlich
und gemüsehändler dungl kam
und weinte bitterlich
und ottokar prohaska kam
und weinte bitterlich
und bernhard röhrig von röhrig und co. kam
und weinte bitterlich
und anton ast, dentist, täglich ausser sonnabend
      von 9–12 and 2–6, kam
und weinte bitterlich
und trude weitz kam
und weinte bitterlich
und edi ritter kam
und weinte bitterlich
und rudi vacek kam
und weinte bitterlich

and frau director reichert came
and cried bitterly
and greengrocer dungl came
and cried bitterly
and ottokar prohaska came
and cried bitterly
and bernhard röhrig of röhrig and co. came
and cried bitterly
and anton ast, dentist, daily except saturday
    from 9–12 and 2–6, came
and cried bitterly
and trude weitz came
and cried bitterly
and edi ritter came
and cried bitterly
and rudi vacek came
and cried bitterly

Aus deinem Himmel von sanften
Erfüllungen
hinweggenommen in Labyrinthe
unausgesprochener Gedanken und Wünsche
gekreuzt von wolkendichten Schlachtschiffen
mit ungewöhnlicher
Munition:
die nicht-erinnerbare Liebe

die nicht-erinnerbare Liebe kreuzt
lautlos in den blauen Buchten
meines Herzens.

Eine Fuszreise ohne Ende
eine Pilgerfahrt auf den Knien
alle Wege sind bestreut mit Dornen
die Fluszläufe die ich durchqueren musz
habe ich selbst geweint.

Aber deine flüsternde Stimme trägt mich fort
und die beinah verwehte Fuszspur
deiner Liebe.

FRIEDERIKE MAYRÖCKER

(1 9 2 4 –   )

An early figure in the Vienna Group, more recently associated with the Graz writers and a founding member of the Graz Authors' Collective, Friederike Mayröcker has long been a figure in the Austrian literary avant garde.

Mayröcker works in several genres. She is known for her radio plays with Jandl—*Der Gigant* [The giant] (1968), *Spaltungen* [Cleavings] (1970), and *Fünf Mann Menschen* [Five man men] (1972). She has also written stories, plays, art criticism, and children's books. But Friedericke Mayröcker is most productive, and perhaps most original, as a poet; she has published about twenty collections since 1956. Many of her poems are experiments in *Konkretismus* or montage poems; some of the later, and more fully "concrete" poems are virtually untranslatable. Her selected poems (*Ausgewalte Gedichte*) appeared in 1979, and the most recent sampler of her work is *Ein Lesebuch* [A reader], of the same year.

———

From your heaven of tender
fulfillments
carried off into labyrinths
of unspoken thoughts and wishes
through which cloudy battleships cruise
with unusual
ammunition,
the love that I can't remember

the love that I can't remember cruises
silently into the blue bays
of my heart.

———

An endless journey by foot
a pilgrimage on the knees
all paths have been strewn with thorns
the rivers that I have to cross
are made of my tears.

But your whispering voice leads me on
and the nearly faded footprints
of your love.

Im Elendsquartier

Im Elendsquartier
wo du mir Cummings vorliest
und ich dir Gertrude Stein
auf dem Drudenfusz stehend
dir den Rücken kehrend
die Rauchsäule des begeisterten Geists
steigt kerzengerade:
act 1 scene 1 scene 5
im Elendsquartier
unter dem Dach
um die Ecke dort
wo noch die letzte Wasserleitung rinnt
spielt einer Harmonika
und ich gehe mit dem Wasserkrug
ganz nah an seine helle Tür
er spielt Harmonika
du spielst Klavier
auf einem imaginären Instrument
im Elendsquartier
hier bei mir
verbreitet sich rasch die Wärme
nebenan kommt einer heim
ob er glücklich ist
er läutet und streift dabei seine Schuhe ab
könntest du dieser heimkehrende Mann sein
und ich an der hellen Tür innen
hier im Elendsquartier
zischt das Wasser
und die Uhr tickt
und der Wodka von gestern nacht
steht in der Flasche
durch meine Finger flieszen
deine blonden Haare
hier im Elendsquartier
vier Treppen hoch
nisten die Wintertauben
im Elendsquartier
hoch oben in der Nähe des Sturms
spreche ich Cummings nach
the goatfooted balloonman and etcetera
und wünsche mir dasz du kommst

In the Slums

In the slums
where you read e. e. cummings to me
and I read Gertrude Stein to you
standing in the pentagram
with my back to you
the smoke column of animated thought
rises as straight as a candle:
act 1 scene 1 scene 5
in the slums
under the roof
around the corner
where the faucet still drips
someone plays an accordion
and I walk carrying the water jug
near his bright door
he plays an accordion
you play the piano
on an imaginary instrument
in the slums
here next to me
the warmth spreads quickly
someone comes home next door
who knows whether he's happy
he rings the bell and wipes his shoes
could this man coming home be you
and I behind the bright door
here in the slums
water hisses
and the clock ticks
and last night's vodka
is in the bottle
your blond hair
flows through my fingers
here in the slums
four flights up
the winter pigeons are nesting
in the slums
high up near the storm
I say after cummings
the goat-footed balloonMan and etcetera
and wish you would come

Tage in der Spindel einen alten Sommers
Tage mit brüchigen grau-pfeifenden Tieren
reglosen Globen
matten Alpen

meine Arme sind ein queres Holz
ich hebe meine Augen
o wie ich dich finde:
in seitlichen Gestirnen
in hohlen Lüften
in verherrlichten Kulissen

eingewachsen ins Nagelbett der Erde
sind wir für alle Zeit
und sie suchen uns vergebens
zwischen den Tannen
in den sanften Muscheln
über den Zacken der Meere
wo mit den Fluten der Trauer sich ans Land werfen
Matrosen und Fische Boote Beeren und Algen

————

Durch die Gitterstäbe meines Herzens
scheint die Welt mir seltsam fremd

auf und nieder hier und dorthin
doch die Tore sind versperrt

immer kleiner sind die Kreise
immer mutloser der Ausbruch

manchmal bleiben Menschen stehen

werfen ein paar leise Worte
werfen einen Blick herein

seltener kommst du vorbei

du hast meine Tür verriegelt
du hast alles abgesperrt

manchmal wirfst du eine Rose
wie ein Stückchen rohes Fleisch

im Vorübergehn herein.

Days on the spindle of a past summer
days with brittle gray-whistling animals
motionless globes
dull Alps

my arms are crossed wood
I lift up my eyes
o how I find you:
in sideways stars
in hollow breezes
in exalted settings

we have grown used to the nail-bed of earth
for all time
and they look for us in vain
between fir trees
in soft mussels
over the ridges of the seas
where sailors fishes boats berries and weeds
are cast ashore by the tides of grief

———

Through the bars of my heart
the world looks very odd

up and down here and there
but the gates are closed

the circles grow smaller and smaller
there's less and less courage to escape

sometimes people stop

whisper a few words
cast a glance inside

you walk past less often

you've locked my door
you've locked up everything

sometimes you throw in a rose
like a piece of raw meat

as you pass by.

mein gedicht

mein gedicht:
ein alltagsgolgotha
auf einsamen heidnischen dorfstraßen
kain vergast
abel vergast
wie die angst von nagasaki
eingeätzt in japanische kirschblüten
mein gedicht:
gewachsen in der schuppenhaut der piranhas
die das tafelgeschirr leerfressen
von leichenstücken
mein gedicht:
ein gesang der stumm bleibt für eurydike
für immer

ne pas se pencher en dehors

ne pas se pencher en dehors
e pericoloso sporgersi
NICHT HINAUSLEHNEN
mein freund—
die messer des fahrtwindes
kappen
deinen kopf wie ein tau
ne pas se pencher en dehors
sei brav bleib im zug
leg an die zügel der vernunft

WALTER BUCHEBNER

(1929–1964)

Born in Mürzzuschlag in Steiermark in 1929, Walter Buchebner was remarkably prolific in his short career as a poet. Suffering from cancer, he announced his death in Paris exactly one year beforehand, then committed suicide on September 4, 1964.

Buchebner was associated with the poets of both Vienna and Graz. His poems were collected in *Zeit aus Zellulose* [Time out of cellulose] in 1969, and other poems, along with his writings and graphics, in *Lyrik, Prosa, Grafik* in 1976.

my poem

my poem:
an everyday golgotha
on lonely heathen village roads
cain gassed
abel gassed
like the fear of nagasaki
etched in japanese cherry blossoms
my poem:
grown between the scales of piranhas
that clean the plates
of pieces of corpses
my poem:
a song for eurydice
that remains mute
forever

ne pas se pencher en dehors

ne pas se pencher en dehors
e pericoloso sporgersi
DON'T LEAN OUT THE WINDOW
my friend—
the knives of the rushing air
will chop off your head
as a wire would
ne pas se pencher en dehors
be good and stay inside the train
put on the reins of common sense

e pericoloso sporgersi
nur menschen ohne verstand
strecken den kopf zwischen den messern
den sternen entgegen—
NICHT HINAUSLEHNEN!

lösch aus die hyazinthe

lösch aus den mond
der erinnerung
die hyazinthe aus edelstahl
der schlamm frißt
was ich ausspeie
es geht nicht an
daß wir das gedächtnis stimmen
wie ein klavier
morgen wird sich
das zimmer mit bissigen stubenfliegen
füllen
morgen kauf ich
in irgendeinem laden
die spaltpilzsuppe
damit stopf ich mir
das maul voll
wie eine frau
die ihren mann satt hat
der sie betrügt

ich bin zur liebe nicht fähig

ich bin zur liebe nicht fähig
ich werde untergehen
ich sehe ein schmutziges meer
schon ganz nahe
ich füttere das meer mit pillen
wie ein huhn ein schwein einen hasen
ich werde das meer schlachten
und sein blut trinken
ich bin zur liebe nicht fähig
ich werde untergehen

ich bin zur liebe nicht fähig
ich werde untergehen

e pericoloso sporgersi
only fools
stretch their heads between knives
to reach the stars—
DON'T LEAN OUT THE WINDOW

extinguish the hyacinth

extinguish the moon
of memory
the steel hyacinth
that gobbles up the slime
that i spit out
it won't do
for us to tune memory
like a piano
tomorrow
the room will be filled
with rabid flies
tomorrow i'll buy
fungus soup
in some store
and i'll stuff it
down my gullet
like a woman
who's fed up
with the husband
who cheats on her

i'm incapable of loving

i'm incapable of loving
i'll go under
i see a dirty sea
very close now
i feed pills to the sea
as to a chicken a pig a rabbit
i'll slaughter the sea
and drink its blood
i'm incapable of loving
i'll go under

i'm incapable of loving
i'll go under

ich werde durch eine tür gehen
aus hitze und sand
ich werde in das feuer gehen
und schmelzen zu eis
ich werde spurlos verlöschen
wie benzin
ich werde untergehen
ich bin zur liebe nicht fähig

i'll go through a door
made of heat and sand
i'll walk into the fire
and melt into ice
i'll vanish without a trace
like gasoline
i'll go under
i'm incapable of loving

———

Weiß
ist die tiefere Farbe des Schweigens
schwerelos
ohne Schatten
und ohne Erinnerung

Eine Ebene Licht
zwischen Himmel und Erde

Hinter den Blumen und Kerzen
hinter dem Rauch der Maroniverkäufer
die Schritte
die nichts mehr berühren

Kein Tor führt hinüber
Kein Weg herauf durch den Schnee—

Ohne Schwere
das Schwebende Weiße
die Ebene Licht zwischen Heimkehr und Traum

———

ALOIS HERGOUTH

(1925 –)

One of the several Styrian poets who have come to prominence since the war, Alois Hergouth, then an assistant at the University of Graz, was awarded the Prize for Poetry in Graz in 1956. Subsequently he became one of the founders of "Forum Stadtpark" in 1960. But Hergouth, never an experimentalist, soon found himself not to be working in the same manner as the other Forum poets and withdrew from the Graz circle.

Hergouth has published six collections of his poetry since 1958, and he is well known as a translator as well as a poet. One of his own collections, *Sladka Gora—Der Süsse Berg* [The sugar mountain] (1965), appeared in Slovene and German. Also important is *Stationen im Wind* [Stations in the wind] (1973). Hergouth's most rec nt collection is *Flucht zu Odysseus* [Flight to Odysseus] (1975).

———

White
is the deeper shade of silence
weightless
without shadow
and without memory

A plane of light
between heaven and earth

Behind flowers and candles
behind the smoke of the chestnut-seller
the footsteps
no longer touching anything

No gateway leads anywhere
no way up through the snow

Without weight
the hovering whiteness
the plane of light between homecoming and dreams

———

Aber die Krähen
die schwarzen Beschwörer
durchbrechen den Bann

in den Nebel geschrieben
ins starrende Eisfell der Bäume geduckt—

schwarze Flammen
aus Flügeln und Augen

sie locken die Wölfe
sie rufen die heulenden Hunde herbei

mitten im Weißen
das Schwarz
das Schwarz
das mit Krallen und Schnäbeln
die Stille zerhackt

———

Die Nacht
hat die Wölfe begraben
festgefroren
verschüttet die Stapfen

die Opfer zu Tode gehetzt
wie die Mörder
der Blutgeruch Angst
in zerrissenen Lefzen vereist

Es ist keine Beute

Blind
von Nacht und von Schnee
der Mondflug
die Flucht
in todlose Stille

———

Träume
Gebete
Gespräche nach innen—

But the crows
black conjurers
break the spell

etched in the fog
in the lurking ice-fur of the trees

black flames
of eyes and wings

they attract the wolves
they call out to howling dogs

in the midst of the whiteness
the blackness
the blackness
that tears apart the silence
with claws and beaks

Night
has buried the wolves
has frozen them stiff
has covered their tracks

has hunted victims to death
like their murderers
the blood-smell of fear
is frozen in their torn lips

There is no prey

Blind from night and snow
the moon-flight
the flight
into deathless silence

Dreams
prayers
talking to one's self

von Spiegel zu Spiegel gelöst
das Echo
der Schattenworte

von Spiegel zu Spiegel
die schwarzen und
weißen
Formeln des Schweigens

from mirror to mirror
echoes
detached shadows of words

from mirror to mirror
black
and white
patterns of silence

Variationen über den Tod

1
Verschließe die Tür.
Doch offen bleibe das Fenster.
Du gehst—gehst für immer.
Laß deinen Atem,
laß deinen Schlaf nicht zurück.
Die Wärme der Hand,
den Glanz des Gefühls,
die Liebe, die Schönheit
löse ab von den Dingen.
Der Raum soll erkalten.
Niemand rühre
Vergessenes an.

2
Nach vielem Wandern
fand ich dein Haus,
    Tod,
fand ich dein schwarzes,
kühl schattendes Haus.
Es erinnerte mich

KURT KLINGER

(1928–   )

Born in Linz in 1928 and conscripted into the German air force at sixteen during the war, Kurt Klinger later was detained in a work camp from which he escaped in 1945. After the war he studied dramatic theory and German at the University of Vienna. Upon completion of his studies he took his first position as a dramaturg in Linz and later continued his directorial apprenticeship in Rome and Düsseldorf. Klinger has since traveled widely throughout Germany and Switzerland, directing in various theaters. Today he lives in Vienna and is a member of the Austrian P.E.N. Club.

   Klinger has also established a considerable reputation as a playwright; at least a dozen of his plays have been successfully staged. And as his presence in this collection suggests, he has also met with success as a poet. His first poems appeared in *Harmonie aus Blut* [Harmony from blood] in 1951, and later poems have been published in *Auf der Erde zu Gast* [A guest on this earth] (1956) and *Entwurf einer Festung* [Design for a fortress] (1970). His poems were collected in *Auf dem Limes* [On the limes] in 1980. Best known as a man of the theater, Kurt Klinger has found time to establish himself as a remarkably speculative poet.

Variations on Death

1
Close the door.
But leave the window open.
You go—go forever.
Don't leave your breath,
don't leave your sleep behind.
The warmth of a hand,
the glow of feelings,
love, beauty,
free yourself of those things.
The space should grow cold.
No one should touch
that which has been forgotten.

2
After much wandering
I found your house,
      Death,
found your dark,
cool, shady house.
It reminded me

an verlassene Schlösser
an der Loire.

Hohe Gittertore stieß ich auf,
Gittertore,
geschmiedet aus Urteil und Gnade,

Und trat in den Park,
    Tod,
nach vielem Wandern
in deinen schwarzen,
feucht schimmernden Park.
Er erinnerte mich
an leergelittne,
gebrochene Augen.

Fand unter Pappeln dann
den einen,
immer verschwiegenen Brunnen.

Nach vielem Wandern
beugte ich mich über das Wasser,
    Tod,
über das schwarze,
grundlos ruhende Wasser.
Es erinnerte mich
an Vollendetes,
jenseits von . . . .

3
Geheimnisvoll blind
tritt die Nacht
durchs Dickicht der Amselrufe.

Brausende Geniste
baute der Wind in den Kronen—
nun schweigt er.

Grau sinkt,
wie Wimpernschatten, der Tod
auf mondkalte Wiesen.

Es haucht mich hinüber.

of deserted castles
on the Loire.

I pushed open the great wrought-iron gates,
wrought-iron gates
forged from judgment and grace,

And stepped into the park,
    Death,
after much wandering
into your dark,
damp, shimmering park.
It reminded me
of broken eyes
emptied of suffering.

And then found under poplars
the one
ever-silent spring.

After much wandering
I bent over the waters,
    Death,
over the black,
bottomless, motionless waters.
They reminded me
of the perfection
on the other side of . . . .

3
Mysteriously blind
the night moves through
the thicket of the blackbirds' cries.

The wind built
roaring nests in the treetops—
now it is silent.

As gray as eye shadow
Death sinks
onto moon-cold meadows.

It wafts me across.

Gefangen

Der Rabe schreit.
    Er hat mich gefangen.
Immer muß ich in seinem Schrei
    durch das Land ziehn.
Der Rabe schreit.
    Er hat mich gefangen.
Gestern saß er im Acker und fror
    und mein Herz mit ihm.
Immer schwärzer wird mein Herz,
    denn es ist von schwarzen Flügeln
zugedeckt.

THOMAS BERNHARD

(1 9 3 1 –   )

Born in Heerlen, Holland, Thomas Bernhard came with his family to Carinthia at an early age. He studied music and drama in Vienna and Salzburg, and has since worked as a reporter, journalist, critic, poet, and dramatist. Today he is certainly among Austria's most distinguished, and most original writers.

Bernhard is greatly influenced by both Trakl and Kafka; his poems are dark, death-obsessed, and surreal. Like many Austrian writers he began his literary career as a poet with collections: in 1957, *Auf der Erde und in der Hölle* [On earth and in hell], and in 1958, *In hora Mortis* and *Unter die Eisen des Mondes* [Beneath the iron of the moon]. His fiction—notably *Frost* (1963), *Verstoerung* [Gargoyles] (1967), and *Das Kalkwerk* [The lime works] (1973)—won him the Austrian State Prize in 1967. But Bernhard is perhaps best known for his violent but Beckett-like plays—*Die Macht der Gewohnheit* [The force of habit] (1973), adapted from his own novel of that name, and the strangely fantastic *Ein Fest für Boris* [A celebration for Boris] (1970).

Described by Harald Gröhler as "a notorious loner," Bernhard resigned from the Austrian P.E.N. Club some years ago. But he has also ignored—and has been ignored by—the Graz Group. His long autobiography (in several parts) has helped to establish him as very much an isolated figure among Austrian writers, the cynic-poet who prefers to go his own way alone.

Bernhard has been extensively translated into English. In addition to *Gargoyles, The Lime Works,* and *The Force of Habit,* his recent novel, *Korrektur* [Galley proofs] (1975), has appeared in English translation as *Correction* (1979). Thomas Bernhard has also written scripts for two feature-length films. In recent years he has devoted much time to writing for the stage; a half-dozen plays have been published, notably, *Immanuel Kant* in 1978 and *Der Weltverbesserer* [The do-gooder] in 1979. Bernhard has also written short prose pieces, in *Der Stimmenimitator* [The ventriloquist] (1979), and *Die Billigesser* [The cheap eaters] (1980). His short stories were collected in 1979 in *Die Erzählungen* [The stories]. Bernhard's memoirs, *Wittgensteins Neffe* [Wittgenstein's nephew], appeared in 1983, and his novel, *Concrete,* was published by Knopf in 1984.

Imprisoned

The raven shrieks.
    He has captured me.
I must go through the land forever
    in his cry.
The raven shrieks.
    He has captured me.
Yesterday he perched in the fields and froze,
    and my heart with him.
My heart blackens more and more
    because it is enfolded
in his black wings.

Kein Baum

Eine Ursache für John Donne

Kein Baum
wird dich verstehn,
kein Wald,
kein Fluß,

kein Frost,
nicht Eis, nicht Schnee,
kein Winter, Du,
kein Ich,

Kein Sturmwind
auf der Höh, kein Grab,
nicht Ost, nicht West,
kein Weinen, weh—
kein Baum . . . .

Müde

Ich bin müde . . . .
Mit den Bäumen führte ich Gespräche.
Mit den Schafen litt ich die Dürre.
Mit den Vögeln sang ich in Wäldern.
Ich liebte die Mädchen im Dorf.
Ich schaute hinauf zur Sonne.
Ich sah das Meer.
Ich arbeitete mit dem Töpfer.
Ich schluckte den Staub auf der Landstraße.
Ich sah die Blüten der Melancholie auf dem Feld meines Vaters.
Ich sah den Tod in den Augen meines Freundes.
Ich streckte die Hand aus nach den Seelen der Ertrunkenen.
Ich bin müde . . . .

Aschermittwoch

Ich möchte hinausgehen
    nach der Nacht,
und meine Hände und meine Lippen
    reinigen,
ich möchte mich reinigen
    an der Sonne und
an den Gräsern—

No Tree
A reason for John Donne

No tree
will understand you,
no forest,
no river,

No frost,
neither ice nor snow,
no winter, you,
no I,

No storm wind
in high places, no grave,
neither east nor west,
no tears, alas,
no tree . . . .

Tired

I'm tired . . . .
I spoke to the trees.
I suffered through the drought with the sheep.
I sang in the forests with the birds.
I loved the girls in the village.
I looked up at the sun.
I saw the sea.
I worked with the potter.
I swallowed the dust of country roads.
I saw the blossoms of melancholy in my father's field.
I saw death in the eyes of my friend.
I reached out for the souls of the drowned.
I'm tired . . . .

Ash Wednesday

I'd like to go out
      after the night
and cleanse my hands
      and my lips,
I'd like to cleanse myself
      with the sun
and with the fields—

Aber es regnet,
und meine Gräser
    sind braun
und alt—

But it is raining
and my fields are brown
and old—

der bestie die das einhorn ritt

nun wirf dem einhorn seine zügel über
steig aus dem blutgen bügel in den tränensee
und spüle fuß und hand

dann steck die ringe an
die knochenspangen
den dunkelsten granat der toten jüdin

so machst du treblinka zu einem fest

sie ziehn schon deine fahne auf
die weiße rune
sie singen schon das feuerzauberlied
bald wird der junge rauch dein blondhaar krönen
stahlblau an deiner hüfte blinkt der tod

die fremden leuchter brennen deinem tanz
du tanzt ihn leicht und stolz zum schlag
der peitschen
den großen erdebetten lang von treblinka

du denkst an erika
das kleine blümelein das auf der heide blüht
und küßt die rüden

dein ist all land wo asche liegt
wo du die heilgen tafeln brachst zum grabgestein

CONNY HANNES MEYER

(1931 –)

Born in Vienna in 1931, Conny Hannes Meyer was interned with other Jewish children by the Nazis. He managed to survive the war and the years afterward, and he began writing poetry in 1947, when he was wandering about Austria, West Germany, and Switzerland, and working at various menial jobs. Today Meyer directs his own dramatic company, Die Komödianten (the Comedians), whose home is the Künstlerhaus in Vienna.

Conny Hannes Meyer remains today a noteworthy poet. His poems were collected in *den mund von schlehen bitter, lyrik* [the mouth bitter from blackthorns, lyrics] in 1960. He has also written several plays which have been performed by Die Komödianten.

the beast that rode the unicorn

let go of the unicorn's reins
and step from the bloodied stirrups into a sea of tears
and wash feet and hands

then put the rings
on the bone joints
the darkest garnet of the dead jewess

thus you make a feast of treblinka

they hoist your flag
the white symbol
they are already singing the magic fire-song
soon the fresh smoke will crown your blond hair
death glitters steel-blue at your hip

strange lights illuminate your dance
you dance lightly and proudly to the beat
of whips
along the great trenches of treblinka

you're thinking of erika
the little flower that blooms on the heath
and kisses the dog pack

yours are all lands where ashes lie
where you break the holy tablets into gravestones

und ist die zeit der goldnen zähne
die du dem sohne schenkst zum würfelspiel
läßt er sie jagen über sarg und wimpel
und zählt nach jedem wurfe neun

und zählt noch dich dazu
und geht dann schlafen

sein traum der schöne tod steigt zu ihm nieder
du winkst ihm zu
er reicht dir seine hände

so wiegt er kühl mit dir sich über treblinka
der toten heide mit dem weißen gras
hin über dem nie wieder weiden stehn weil da
das einhorn alle blüte fraß und alle spur

von der geliebten karawane

im buche der eisernen engel stand nichts
von verbotenen nelken und sternen

so gingen hervor aus der guten hand Gottes
die trugen ihr flammendes merkmal

sie trugen den sand aus der wüste im haar
und er war ihre bittere speise

sie aßen ihn schweigend er war ihre krone
am morgen am abend er war ihre zeit

oft gruben sie nachts nach den tieferen steinen
doch brannte für sie nie ein dornbusch

kein führender stab aus geheiligtem ahorn
ging vor ihnen her nach gomorrha

sie gingen allein

sie folgten den tüchern der schwermut
ihr blut in den goldenen krügen
die tränen in denen aus steingut

it is the time of the golden teeth
which you give to your son to use as dice
he throws them over coffin and flag
counting nine at each throw

and it still includes you
and then he goes to sleep

his dream of beautiful death descends to him
you beckon to him
he offers you his hands

and calmly he rocks with you over treblinka
the dead heath with the white grass
on which there will never again be meadows
since the unicorn devoured all buds and traces

of the beloved caravan

in the book of the iron angels there is nothing
of forbidden carnations and stars

thus those who bore the flaming mark
came forth from the right hand of God

they wore the desert sand in their hair
and sand was their bitter nourishment

they silently ate it and it was their crown
morning and evening were their times

they dug at night for the deeper stones
but no bush ever burned for them

no sanctified staff of maple
went before them toward gomorrah

they went alone

they followed shrouds of melancholy
their blood in golden jars
their tears in jars of clay

so gingen sie tage um tage und barfuß
in nächten nicht weniger stumm nach gomorrha
als jene die vor ihnen gingen und bloß

gesellten sich schlangen zu ihnen die tanzten
und zeigten den weg nach gomorrha dann war er
noch weit und die schlangen sie zeigten ihn wortlos

es kamen auch geier herauf und mit ihnen
sie kreisten am wüstensandhimmel

sie kreisten da schweigsam doch kreisten sie immer
des abends des morgens im dunkel und licht

selten stieg ihnen das zelt eines baumes
empor aus den ewigen dünen

und wenn war es schwarz wie wacholder
dann sahn sie hinauf
der flügelschlag oben jedoch war von geiern
kein bote war da im gezweige

sie trugen das zeichen
sie waren erwählte
sie trugen ihr grab schon im haare
gomorrha ging unter für sie

so day after day they walked on bare feet
they walked to gomorrah through the night
just as mutely as those who had gone before them naked

they were accompanied by serpents that danced
and showed them the way to gomorrah which was far away
and the serpents showed them the way silently

they were joined by vultures
that silently circled the desert sky above

and silently circled yet constantly circled
at evening at morning in darkness and light

the tent of a tree
seldom arose out of the endless dunes

and if it did it was as black as a juniper
and then they looked up
but the beating of wings in the branches
came from vultures and not messengers

they bore the mark
they were chosen
they already bore their grave in their hair
gomorrah was lost for their sake

Der letzte Tropfen Schnee

Der letzte Tropfen Schnee
rinnt von den Marillenzweigen.

Süsser Saft
in roten Ästchen
taut langsam auf.

Die Mutter ruft das Kind
—und das war ich.
Die Brüder toben noch herum.

Ich hör' sie springen
wie die jungen Pferde.
Den Vater hör ich lachen
hinterm Haus. . . .

Heut sind die lieben Brüder
längst schon tot
und nur die Eltern
—schwache Hüllen—leben.

MARGARETHE HERZELE

(1931 –)

Margarethe Herzele, the wife of the painter Günther Kraus, is herself a painter as well as a poet
and novelist. Born in St. Veit an der Glan, she today lives and works alternately in Vienna and in
Carinthia. Herzele's paintings have been exhibited widely throughout Europe and the United
States, and her poems have appeared in various journals in English and in Slovene translation as
well as in German. She has also published her poems in several collections: *Herzele* [Little heart]
(1966), *Schneelieder* [Snow songs] (1970), *Carinthian Love Songs* (1978, in English and Ger-
man), *Reflexionen Gelben Lichts* [Reflections of yellow lights] in 1983, and *Trauer—De dun-
kelste Farbe* [Sadness—the darkest color], also in 1983.

As would be expected, Herzele is an intensely visual poet—a lyric poet of nature, but a poet
whose lyrics expose the dark places made by man as well. And yet her gifts as a narrative poet are
at least as apparent. Herzele is a member of the Austrian P.E.N. Club.

The Last Snowflake

The last bit of snow
melts on the apricot branches.

Sweet sap
in red twigs
slowly thaws.

A mother calls her child
—and that was I.
My brothers are roughhousing.

I hear them jump
like young horses.
I hear father laughing
behind the house. . . .

My dear brothers
have been dead for years
Only my parents—fragile shells—
are still alive.

Mutter Chaos

Mutter.
Mutter Chaos!

Gelbgesattelt reit' ich
auf der stärksten
meiner kleinen
Weinbergschnecken.

Hacke mit den Lattenstöcken
Flirrstreifen in den Maiwind.

Mutter Chaos, Blutmutter, Traummutter,
Stundenschlag- und Einschlafmutter.

Fiebermutter mit der Perle—
kein Zurück mehr.

Übermorgen

Übermorgen kommst du.
Ich wartete
und die Blüte fiel ab
von meinem Leib:
die goldenen Schuppen von den Fingern,
die silbernen Perlen der Haut.

Jetzt bin ich Gemäuer
zersprungener Tempel,
Lianen und Schlangen
halten mich noch.

Kleine Eulen pickten
das gelbe Licht aus meinen Augen.
Wenn es regnet im Dschungel
hocken sie still
an meiner Brust.

März Mondnacht

Er sucht und sucht.
Er geht und geht.

Mother Chaos

Mother,
Mother Chaos.

On a yellow saddle
I ride the sturdiest
of my small snails.

With pickets
I cut strips from the May wind.

Mother Chaos, Blood-Mother, Dream-Mother,
Mother of tolled hours and of sleep.

Fever-Mother with the pearl—
there's no going back.

The Day After Tomorrow

You'll come
the day after tomorrow.
I waited
and the bloom fell away
from my body—
the gold scales from my fingers,
the silver pearls of my skin.

Now I am the walls
of a gutted temple,
still held up
by vines and snakes.

Small owls pecked
the yellow light from my eyes.
When it rains in the jungle
they perch silently
on my breast.

March Moon-Night

He searches and searches.
He walks and walks.

Er horcht und steht—
der Mann mit dem Pelzchen.

Bleiern die Nacht.
Sie frißt den Mond
und wird nicht satt.

Mattglänzend, fahl, antwortlos—
das nackte Land.

Da schlägt er den Himmel
—wuttrommelartig—
doch nichts spürt die Faust!

Nur die Luft durchdringt
scharfzackig grün wie Flaschenglas,
seinen Hals.

Am Ufer des Dschang

Am Ufer des Dschang
steht eine Tote.

Der Wind trägt die Asche ihres Gesichtes fort
und die Hand
zerbröckelt wie Lehm.

Das Wasser ist schwarz, Mulden und Wellen.
Und hinter einem schmutzigen Himmel—
die metallische Scheibe Sonne. . . .

He stops and listens—
the man with the furs.

The night is leaden.
It devours the moon
and remains unsatisfied.

Gleaming dully, sallow, silent—
the naked land.

He strikes at the sky,
drumming angrily,
but his fist feels nothing.

Only the air,
sharp and green like bottle glass,
penetrates at his neck.

On the Banks of the Chang

A dead woman stands
on the banks of the Chang.

The wind carries the ashes
of her face away
and her hand crumbles like clay.

The water is black, waves and hollows,
And behind the dirty sky
the metallic disc of the sun. . . .

dein Lachen—und Luftballone steigen vom Himmel

der Schneeball, den du mir zuwirfst, beginnt schon aufzublühn
du neben mir—und die Taube lehnt an der Schulter des Himmels
das Blatt in deiner Hand spricht ein Gedicht
deine Strähne an meinem Gesicht—ich schenke dir etwas durch das Gitter
   der Kindheit
jede vertane Chance wird noch einmal April

ein taubenspäter Nachmittag

schläfriges Licht des Novemberflügels
im Schnabel die Botschaft des ersten Schnees
das Lächeln versteckt im Gefieder
das Leuchten tritt in sich zurück
alle Zeichen werden ein Schweben
wir tauchen tief in die Dämmerung ein
was geschieht, ist ein Abbild im Spiegel

———

im Schatten des Engels ist es geschehn
das Blatt ist in der Strömung gewachsen
der Flügel hat sich geteilt
das Boot ist dem Engel entgegengelaufen
den Schnabel verhaftet im Blau

JUTTA SCHUTTING

(1937 –   )

Jutta Schutting began her career as a poet late but in excellent company; her first collection, *In der Sprache der Inseln* [In the language of islands] appeared in 1973 with an introduction by Ernst Schönwiese. Schutting has since published two collections of stories, *Parkmord* [Death in the park] (1975), and *Sistiana* (1976). In the latter year another collection of her poems, *Lichtungen* [Illuminations] appeared, and in 1978 she published a mixed-genre collection, *Salzburg retour*, and *Am Morgen von der Reise* [On the morning of the trip], an account of the growth of two children. Schutting also writes for children.

Often associated with Christine Busta and Christine Lavant, Jutta Schutting is better understood as a remote, reflective, and highly individual poet of striking originality. Schutting is one of the more atypical members of the Graz Authors' Collective.

you laugh—and balloons descend from the sky

the snowball you threw at me begins to bloom
you next to me—the dove leans on Heaven's shoulder
a poem grows from the leaf in your hand
your hair touching my face—
I give you a gift through the fence of childhood
each wasted chance will once again be April

late afternoon doves

drowsy light of November wings
the message of the first snow in their bills
a smile hidden in feathers
brightness withdraws into itself
all signs are suspended
we dive deep into dusk
what occurs now is all reflection

———

it happened in the angel's shadow
a leaf grew in the stream
a wing unfolded
a boat ran against the angel
transfixed the prow in the blue

auf dem Schatten des Engels wird es geschehn
ein Flügel wird beim anderen wachen
die fallende Welle des letzten Blattes
wird noch einmal den Engel hinübertragen
der gelöschte Engel das vorletzte Blatt
die Flügel geschlossen vom Blau

———

gib dem Hund zu trinken, ihn dürstet
wirf das Mondblatt den Brunnen hinab
lass die Welle von der Leine
mach dem Vogel die Flügel auf

zieh mich ins Engelsgras
leg den Teich zu mir
schick beide Quellen miteinander schlafen
deck mich mit Mondsträhne zu

lass uns die blaue Rose machen

———

dort draussen in der Nacht stehen einige Häuser,
die, von traurigen Kindern gezeichnet,
Fensterkreuze vor schwarzen Fahnen sind

dort drunten am Abend stehen einige Häuser,
in deren Fenstern auf der Flucht vor der Nacht
sich der Himmel sammelt

dort drüben am Nachmittag steht ein Haus,
in dessen vier Fenstern
die Reue eines längst gelöschten Brandes
die Versöhnung seiner Bewohner im Fegefeuer
und ein Wort des Propheten Elias lodert

dort droben am Morgen und Mittag und Abend
steht ein Haus, dessen zwei Fenster,
von zwei Engeln aus der Nacht gebrochen,
einander öffnen und schließen

it will happen by the angel's shadow
one wing will watch over the other
the falling wave of the last leaf
will carry the angel across once more
the obliterated angel the penultimate leaf
the wings folded in the blue

———

give water to a thirsty dog
throw a slice of moon down the well
release the wave from its leash
open the wings of a bird

take me to the angel's fields
place the pond next to me
send both springs to bed together
cover me with the moon's pigtails

let's grow a blue rose

———

out there in the night there are houses
drawn by sad children
with black-crossed windows

down there in the evening there are houses
with windows that catch the sky
before night darkens it

over there in the afternoon there's a house—
its four windows blazing with
the sorrow of a long-extinguished fire
the reconciliation of its family in purgatory
and a word from the prophet Elijah

up there, morning, noon, and evening
there's a house whose two windows,
smashed by two angels in the night,
open and close one another

Wie der Wind

Wie der Wind singt,
so klingt kein Lied.

Kein Mensch versteht,
wovon der Fluß spricht.

Erst wenn unsere Ohren
taub sind für unsere Lieder,

werden wir wieder ein Ohr haben
für den Fluß und für den Wind.

In harter Schale

In harter Schale,
ein nahrhafter kern—
schlag ihn auf.

Iß!
Das sind
die Früchte
vom Herbst.

OTTO LAABER

(1934 – 1973)

A poet of great promise, Otto Laaber was born in Klosterneuberg to an ancient farming family of the region. He studied for a time in the United States, then returned to Austria to undertake university study in history and English. But his imagination became obsessed with death, and on the fifteenth of July 1973 he committed suicide.

In his short career Laaber showed great talent as a poet; his poems appeared in *Neue Wege* and in various collections of younger Austrian poets in the early 1970s. In 1976 his poems were posthumously collected in *Inventur* [Inventory]. Laaber was certainly one of the most curiously macabre poets of his own or of any generation.

Like the Wind

No song sounds
the way the wind sings.

No one understands
what the river has to say.

When our ears
become deaf to our songs

we'll again be able to hear
the river and the wind.

In a Hard Shell

In a hard shell,
a nourishing kernel—
break it open.

Eat!
These are
the fruits
of autumn.

Am Feld

Am Feld mußt du stehen,
Spreu in der Hand,
und zusehen, wie die Vögel
sich schwerfressen an der Ernte.

So mußt du stehen,
—selber ein Vogelschreck—
mitten auf deinen
ausgeplünderten
Feldern.

Wer sagt

Wer sagt, daß der Tod
dunkel sein wird?
Ein Grab der Wünsche?
Ein Sack über dem Kopf?
Wenn er vielleicht mit Schellen
kommt und Trompeten,
ein Narr in kariertem Gewand,
ein Tölpel, ein Schelm,
der dich abholt
zu einem ländlichen Fest?

Die Trommel

Bespannt die Trommel
                mit der Haut vom Menschen
damit sie dröhne
                die große Trommel
die Trommel Zeit
                die vom Ruhm Einiger laut redet
Weniger laut von Anderen
                deren Haut nur gut war
die Trommel der Zeit
                zu bespannen

In the Field

You must stand in the field
with chaff in your hands
and watch how the birds
fatten themselves on the harvest.

That's how you must stand
—yourself a scarecrow—
in the middle
of your
plundered
fields.

Who Says

Who says
that death will be dark?
A grave for wishes?
A sack over your head?
Perhaps he'll come wearing bells
and with a fanfare,
a fool in motley,
a lout, a scoundrel
who takes you
to a fine country feast.

The Drum

Cover the drum
    with human skin
so that it resounds
    the great drum
the drum of time
    the great drum
that sounds loudly
    of the fame of some
and less loudly of those
    whose skin served only
to cover
    the drum of time

The New Generation

Dein Urteil steht auf
einer schwarzen Tafel
hingeschrieben von einem Mann mit
ausgelöschter Laterne
zwischen Abfahrt und vier-
undzwanzigstündiger Verspätung
zwischen Verhaftung
und Entlassung erwarten dich
Masken
Ziffern
Finger
laufen zu dir
bemalen dich rot
oder grün
du bist ein Bahnhof
verraten
verschleppt
versteigert—
die Nacht macht keine Erklärungen
für plötzlich
geänderte Reiserouten
die Antennen sind tot
die Koffer sind tot
das Büfett ist eingeschlummert
nur Windhunde ohne Ketten
wahren Distanz

HERMANN GAIL

(1 9 3 9 –   )

Born in Pöggstal in Lower Austria, Hermann Gail as a young man served ten years in an Austrian prison, an experience which is at the center of much of his poetry. He now lives in Vienna, where he works as a freelance writer and runs the David-Presse, a small literary publishing house. Like many Austrian poets, Gail has written in various genres. He made his literary reputation with a novel, *Gitter* [Bars], in 1971, and he has a later novel, *Prater* (1976). His short stories of Vienna were collected in *Liaisons* (1974), and he has written plays for radio as well.

Gail's first collection of poems appeared in 1972 under the title of *Exil ohne Jahrszeiten* [Exile without seasons]. His most recent book, *Weite Herrschaft der weissen Mäuse* [The far dominions of the white mice], was published in 1979.

———

Your sentence
is written
on a blackboard
by a man with
an extinguished lantern
between departure and twenty-
four-hour delay
between arrest
and release
masks
figures
fingers
await you
hurrying toward you
painting you red
or green
you're a railway station
betrayed
dragged away
auctioned off—
night doesn't explain
the sudden detours
the antennas are dead
the suitcases are dead
the refreshment bar is asleep
but the greyhounds without chains
keep their distance

———

Du hast nicht einmal Füße mehr
an deinem Leib
acht Zehen besitzt du in
einem kleinen Schächtelchen
und mit dem Daumen deiner Phantasie
stehst du bereits im
Grab von Chikago

Du hast nicht einmal Angst mehr
Leibowitz verteidigt dich
und bittet um Freispruch

Aber ganz im geheimen
spinnst du an einem Wunsch:
du wirst dir ein
schneeweißes Hemd kaufen

———

Auch ich könnte mir Benzin
in das Knie spritzen
und dann sagen:
mehr als hundert Kilo trage ich nicht

Mir bleibt nichts übrig
als alle Zellen auf meine Schultern zu nehmen
den lauten Schrei
noch lauter zu machen
die scharfe Luft zwischen dem Flackern
deiner riesengroßen Augen einzusaugen

Wisch dir die Uniform weg
wisch dir die Haut weg

———

Ein Zwerg tänzelt auf der Folterbank
Ein Zwerg schreit auf der Folterbank
Ich stehe dicht an der Seite des Zwerges

———

You don't even have feet
attached to you anymore
just eight toes
in a small box
and with the thumb of your imagination
you're already
in a grave in Chicago

You don't even feel fear
Leibowitz is your defense counsel
and pleads for your acquittal

But secretly
you make a wish:
you'll buy yourself
a snow-white shirt

———

I too could inject gasoline
into my knee
and then say,
I can't carry
more than a hundred kilos

There's nothing left
but to carry all the cells
on my shoulders
and to make the loud scream
even louder
to suck in the sharp air
between the flickering
of your enormous eyes

Peel your uniform off
peel your skin away

———

A dwarf hops on the rack
A dwarf screams on the rack
I'm right next to the dwarf

*

Wenn die Nacht kommt
habe ich nichts verrichtet
als gegen die roten Wolken gestarrt
habe mich in ein Tier verwandelt
als Hund einen Menschen nachgeahmt
*

Morgens denke ich manchmal
diese grünen Türen plötzlich geöffnet
führen direkt in die Hölle
Und dann krieche ich hinaus
ein grauer Maulwurf
Meine Hügel sind aber
steinerne Hügel
*

Vielleicht bist du der Bruder der Rose
der die fremde Hand fürchtet
der die Bleikugel fürchtet
der die Stahlrute fürchtet
Vielleicht sind alle Rosen Häftlinge
die auf eine Botschaft von dir warten

*

When night comes
I've done nothing
but stare at the red clouds
I've changed myself into an animal
a dog that imitates humans

*

In the morning I sometimes think
that if these green doors suddenly opened
they'd lead straight to hell
And then I'd crawl out
like a gray mole
but my hills
are rock hills

*

Perhaps you're the brother of the rose
who fears a strange hand
who fears a bullet
who fears a steel rod
Perhaps all roses are prisoners
who wait for a message from you

Wo warst du,
als das geschah,
wußtest du nicht,
daß der Totengräber
vom neuen Jahr sprach,
vom fressenden Schotter,
von der alten Frau,
die man auf den Mann legt,
der schon liegt?

Ich erinnere mich an ein Datum,
da sollte ich den Freund anrufen
und sagen:
«Der Wahnsinn geht weiter,
das Haus wird nicht abgetragen,
die Todesangst feiert Hochzeit."

Er hätte etwas gesagt.

ALFRED KOLLERITSCH

(1931–)

Alfred Kolleritsch was born in Brunnsee, in Styria, in 1931. He studied history and German literature, then wrote a dissertation on Heidegger and undertook a career in teaching in the city of Graz. It was in his course in literature in the Municipal College there in 1960 that "Forum Stadtpark" was born. He edited *manuskripte*, the journal in which the Graz writers often first appeared, and he was elected president of the Group in 1968. Today Kolleritsch is recognized as the founder of the Graz Group and as a shaping influence in contemporary Austrian letters.

One of the Graz writers published by Residenz Verlag, Kolleritsch has written two novels, *Die Pfirsichtöter* [The peach killers] (1972) and *Die grüne Seite* [The green side] (1974). But he is perhaps better known for his poems, which were collected in 1978 in *Einübung in das Vermeidbare* [Practice in evasion]. For this book Kolleritsch was honored with the Petrarch Prize. Kolleritsch has continued his academic work as well, having edited Proceedings and Festschriften for the Academy of Music and Art in Graz.

A taciturn and tentative poet, Kolleritsch has said, "Language can be fiendish; the only hope in living with it is continual practice." Kolleritsch's poetry, hardly typical of that later to be associated with the Graz Group poets, nevertheless seems to set forth the procedures and concerns for several of them, especially Handke.

———

Where were you
when it happened;
didn't you know
that the gravedigger
spoke of the new year,
of the rapacious macadam,
of the old woman
that one puts on top of a man
who's already on his back?

I remember a date
on which I should have called a friend
to say,
"Insanity is on the march,
the house won't be torn down,
the fear of death sets the wedding table."

He would have said something.

Du bist stumm,
ein beendetes Spiel.

————

Es ist nicht so zu verstehen,
wie ich es verstanden habe.

Ich merke,
daß es weitergegangen ist,
ich lebe es schon,
aber ich sage ganz etwas anderes.

Die Arme strecke ich aus,
sie fliegen wie Freesbyscheiben voraus.
Niemand fängt sie.
Ich wische mir nichts aus dem Gesicht.
Ich sitze hier,
spitz
wie die Nadel.

————

Wenn man schreibt,
gehen die Türen nicht zu,
eine Frage klebt an der anderen,
eine Befürchtung
stülpt sich aus der nächsten.

So dringt die Harmonie ein,
wie Eis, das durch Stahl wächst,
und man spürt das warme Rieseln
ringsum.

Dann schmerzen die Augen,
dann zerbricht man das Liebste,
dann ist die Güte ein Würgegriff,
dann schreibt man ins Leere
oder sagt:
«Nur bis an den Rand eines Herzens.»

Man sagt es dir,
vor der man nur eine Hand hat,
sich zu verbergen.

You're silent;
the game's up.

————

It can't be understood
as I have understood it.

I notice
that it has gone on;
I'm already living it
but I'm saying something completely different.

I extend my arms,
they fly out like frisbees.
No one catches them.
I wipe nothing from my face.
I sit here
sharp
as a needle.

————

When one writes
the doors don't close,
one question sticks to another,
fear
unfolds from the next one.

That's how harmony forces its way in,
like ice spreading through steel,
and one feels the warm trickle
all around.

Then the eyes ache,
then one destroys what one loves,
then goodness is a stranglehold,
then one writes in a vacuum,
or says,
"Only up to the margin of the heart."

That's what one says to you,
and one has nothing but a hand
to hide behind.

Daß man sich mitunter einholt,
will sich nachts als Fortschritt
verraten,
die Gedanken kennen den Strom,
der mit anderen Strömen
zuletzt nur den Namen teilt,
wie tief man sich auch in die Dinge stößt.

Was Bilder zurückläßt,
daran erinnern wir uns,
wir hetzen die Erfahrungen
zu Ketten zusammen
und bekennen erschöpft,
wie einig wir sind.

Hingesetzt auf diese Sandbänke,
träumen wir von Steinen.

Occasionally you catch up with yourself
and at night
it is divulged that this
is progress;
your thoughts know the current
that shares only its name
with other currents
no matter how deep you go.

Whatever leaves images behind
we remember;
we chase experiences
into chains
and wearily we realize
how much we agree.

Sitting on these sandbanks
we dream of stones.

Der Rand der Wörter

Wir sitzen am Rand des Feldwegs und reden.
Die größte Not ist lange vorbei, denn am Gletscherrand lagern die Leichen
    ab.
Wer steht am Rand des Feldes, am Rand des Highway?—Cary Grant!
Am Grubenrand liegt, vom Spaten gespalten, ein Engerling.
Der Rand des Schmutzflecks trocknet schon.

PETER HANDKE

(1942–   )

Certainly the best known of the younger Austrian writers, indeed in the United States one of the most celebrated of the radical young German-language writers, Peter Handke was born in Griffen (Carinthia) and, after various educational escapades, studied law at the University of Graz. In 1966 he participated in a "Gruppe 47" conference of German writers, held at Princeton, New Jersey; there he outspokenly attacked the work of his colleagues and thus established himself as the spokesman for the younger generation of German-language writers. But long before 1966 he had become a central figure in the Graz Group, having first published in *manuskripte* and having been discovered there by Alfred Kolleritsch.

But Handke, who lived much of his life abroad—in Düsseldorf, in the United States, and in France—is perhaps best known in these countries as a neo-Brechtian playwright: for his notorious *Publikumsbeschimpfung* of 1966, translated into English as *Offending the Audience;* or for *Kaspar* (1968), Handke's first full-length play, based on the life of Kaspar Hauser; or for *Der Ritt über den Bodensee* [The ride across Lake Constance] (1971). His novels, *Die Hornissen* [The hornets] (1966) and *Der Hausierer* [The peddler] (1967), show something of the influence of William Faulkner and are widely translated and read. In the 1970s came his *Der kurze Brief zum langen Abschied* [Short letter, long farewell] (1972), and *Wunschloses Unglück* (1972), translated as *A Sorrow Beyond Dreams* in 1975. Partly autobiographical narratives (the latter an account of the suicide of Handke's mother), both were essentially conventional in technique.

Handke's novel *Das Gewicht der Welt*, of 1977, was published as *The Weight of the World* by Farrar, Straus & Giroux in 1984. His most recent play, *Über die Dörfer* [Beyond the villages], appeared in the same year, as did his most recent work of fiction, *Kindergeschichte* [Children's history]. A Handke collection in English translation is forthcoming in 1984.

Handke is perhaps less known as such, but is also important as a poet. His poems have appeared in three major collections, *Die Innenwelt der Aussenwelt der Innenwelt* [The inner world of the outer world of the inner world] (1969, 1974), *Deutsche Gedichte* [Poems in German] (1969), and *Als das Wünschen noch geholfen hat* (1974, translated as *Nonsense and Happiness* in 1976). A set of poems in our selection is taken from a sequence published in 1976, *Das Ende des Flanierens* [An end to idling].

The Edge of Words

We sit at the edge of the field-path and talk.
The time of greatest want has passed long ago
   since corpses now lie at the glacier's edge.
Who's standing at the edge of the field,
   at the edge of the highway? Cary Grant!
A larva lies at the edge of the pit, split by a shovel.
The edge of the stain is already drying.

Es wird bitter kalt, und dem Captain Scott fängt die Wunde vom Rand her
    zu eitern an.
Am Rand der Erschöpfung reden wir alle in Hauptsätzen.
Von den schmutzigen Taschen des Toten haben die
    Fingernägel des Plünderers einen Rand.
Wir sitzen am Rand des Feldwegs, am Rand des
    Feldes, und reden, und reden.
Wo der Rand der Wörter sein sollte, fängt trockenes
    Laub an den Rändern zu brennen an, und die Wörter
    krümmen sich unendlich langsam in sich selber:
"Diese Trauerränder!"
Dieser Rand der Trauer.

aus *Das Ende des Flanierens*

1
Dürftiges Alleinsein:
Kälte
Nacht
Belag auf den Lippen
Niedergeschlagene Augen

2
In der nieselnden Finsternis des Boulevards
an dich denkend
spüre ich die Innenseiten meiner Hände
heiß werden
im Bedürfnis dich zu umfassen
in Gedanken kratze ich dir die Kleider
herunter
um dir näher zu sein

3
Wir tun als ob das Alleinsein ein Problem sei
Vielleicht ist es eine fixe Idée—
wie die Angst, im Sommer zu sterben
wenn man schneller verwest

7
Drei Totenschädel:
Im Café sitzen drei Burschen
und haben ihre Sturzhelme
(mit offenem Visier)
neben sich auf den Boden gestellt

It's getting as cold as ice, and the edge of Captain Scott's wound is
    beginning to suppurate.
We all use principal clauses when we are on the edge of exhaustion.
The edges of the plunderer's fingernails have become soiled from the dirty
    pockets of the corpse.
We sit at the edge of the field-path and talk and talk.
At the place where the edges of the words should be
    dry foliage begins to burn at the edges, and the words
    curve infinitely slowly into themselves:
"These mourning-edges!"
This edge of mourning.

from *An End to Idling*

1
Shabby loneliness
Cold
Night
Lips coated
Eyes downcast

2
In the drizzling darkness of the boulevard
thinking of you
I feel my palms
become hot
with a desire to hold you
and I imagine myself tearing your clothes
off
in order to be closer to you

3
We act as if being alone were a problem
Perhaps it is an *idée fixe*—
like the fear of dying in summer
when one decays more quickly

7
Three death's heads:
Three young punks
They sit in the café
their crash helmets
(with open visors)
beside them on the floor

8
Die Arme reckend:
Herrlich ist das Leben heute! (Pause.)
Und irgendwo stirbt wieder einer
auf die unverschämteste Weise—
Bei der Vorstellung von dem allgemeinen
höllischen Tod
in einer engen Straße stehenbleiben
und das Wort «tragisch" erleben

11
He, du an der Straßenecke:
die Geschichte von der Einsamkeit des
modernen Menschen
kennen wir ja inzwischen
Nun verschwinde auch du nachts von den
windigen Straßenecken!

12
Schöne Unbekannte mit dem breiten Gesicht,
die du drinnen im Restaurant an der
Zigarette ziehst:
Im Vorbeigehen auf der Straße
erkenne ich dein Gesicht
und es wird undeutlich,
aufblühend in meiner Erinnerung

        17
        Zufrieden mit einer Arbeit
        gehst du ins Café
        Du stehst an der Musicbox
        und an der Theke steht eine Frau
        mit weißen Stiefeln
        Und eigentlich müßte dieses Gedicht
        jetzt weitergehen

8
You stretch your arms out:
life's wonderful today! (Pause.)
And somewhere someone's dying again
in the most shameless way—
When you think how universal
this horrible death is
you stop in a narrow street
and learn what the word "tragic" means

11
Hey, you on the corner,
we already know
the story
of the loneliness of modern man
So don't stand there all night
on that windy corner!

12
Stranger, beauty with the broad face,
drawing on your cigarette
there in the restaurant
As I pass on the street
I recognize that face of yours
and it will become unclear
when it blooms in my memory

17
Satisfied with the work that you've done
you enter a café
You stand in front of the jukebox
and a girl
in white boots
is standing at the bar
And really this poem should
be continued

Intermezzo: Zu Mittag im Bazar-Café

Der Himmel wird schwarz
von der Sonne
bezieht sich meinen geschlossenen Augen
mit finstersten Wolken
Musik türkisch
im Hintergrund
die Sonne
verbrennt mein Gesicht
& ich
schlafe fast ein

(Neptun, den 11. August 1975)

———

Poate,
Nu vom mai fi nici! . . .
Ion Minulescu
Immer die Frage nach Liebe was ist das immer wieder die
Suche nach Identität mit dem Andern der Andern sie gibts
nicht die Sehnsucht sie bleibt oder es muß der Tod sein

GERALD BISINGER

(1 9 3 6 –)

Born in Vienna and educated at the university there (he studied psychology and Italian literature) Gerald Bisinger made his first literary reputation as poetry editor of *Neue Wege,* a publication for young Austrian writers, where he served from 1962 to 1970.

Bisinger now lives in Berlin, but he is closely associated with the Graz poets. He is known as an experimentalist, most recently with prose techniques in poetry. He is also very much influenced by H. C. Artmann, a writer whom he has edited and about whom he has written. Bisinger is also a translator, especially of Italian poetry.

Gerald Bisinger's own poems have appeared in a number of collections, beginning with *Zikaden und Genever* [Cicadas and gin] in 1963. Later he published 7 *Gedichte zum Vorlesen* [7 poems to be read aloud] (1968) and 5 *kurze Gedichte für Kenner* [5 short poems for specialists] in the same year. A third collection by Bisinger in 1968 was *Ein Drachenteufel & hinterhältig* [A dragon-devil & insidious]. In Turin in 1971 Bisinger's 7 *neue Gedichte / 7 nuove poesie* [7 new poems] appeared in a bilingual edition. Bisinger also edited the definitive collection of H. C. Artmann's poetry. The most recent collection of Bisinger's own poems is entitled *Poema ex ponto* [Poems *ex ponto*] of 1977. Since 1973 he has served on the managing board of the Graz Authors' Collective.

Intermezzo: Noon in the Bazaar Café

The sky becomes black
from the sun
and covers my closed eyes
with the darkest clouds
Turkish music
in the background
the sun
burns my face
& I
almost fall asleep

(Neptune, August 11, 1975)

Poate,
Nu vom mai fi nici! . . .
Ion Minulescu
Always the question about love what is it again and again the
search for identity with the other of another it doesn't
exist longing stays with you or it has to be death

absolut einsam oder unio mystica mit dem einzig mög-
lichen Partner Ende jeden Bewußtseins so ist jeder ein
Partner und richtig als faulender Fraß für Gewürm oder
Asche Asche zu Asche amorph die Gestaltung ist leben ist
Kompromiß provisorisch bis hin zum Tod der absolut ist so-
eben hab ich auf deutsch dieses Gedicht niedergeschrieben
das Minulescu neunzehnhundertunddreizehn erstmals rumänisch
veröffentlicht hat ich zitiere es hier lese es jetzt noch einmal

(Neptun, den 12. August 1975)

Epilog in Berlin

Irgendwie bin ich froh wieder hier zu sein in der Groß-
räumigkeit dieser Stadt mit dem dichten Verkehrsnetz
in dem lauen Licht das nicht wider die Augäpfel drückt
wenn sie schutzlos sind unter der Sonne die hier nicht
verbrennt mit Rührung bin ich S-Bahn gefahren sah ich
neben dem Bahndamm die Goldraute blühn etwa vor einem
Jahr hat Ludwig Harig dieser Pflanze größte Beachtung
geschenkt mit Rührung aber und nicht ohne Sehnsucht ge-
denk ich der beiden Türken dort im Bazar-Café zu Nep-
tun die im erhitzten Sand in metallener Wanne mit den
Kännchen rührten bis er fertig war der Café

Mit der Rührung des Wiederfindens sah ich die Grune-
wald-Kiefern von der S-Bahn aus und ich dachte nicht
erinnern sie mehr an die Kiefern in Oberöstreich die
meiner Jugend der Kindheit heute erinnerten sie an
sich selbst und ich dachte bin ich tatsächlich hei-
misch geworden in dieser Stadt am S-Bahnhof Wannsee
als ich Rasierwasser kaufte traf ich Flavia sonnen-
gebräunt sie war auf Elba und vom Büro aus schickte
ich dann Gedichte von mir auf deutsch an die blonde
Natascha die nicht deutsch kann weithin nach Nep-
tun und nach London schrieb ich rumänisch an Vera

Ich sitze am Eßtisch in meiner eigenen Wohnung trink
Rotwein schreib diese Zeilen neben mir steht mein Tele-
fon soeben hat mich Angelika angerufen ich unterbrach
diese Strofe und glaub auch daß ich sie nicht mehr be-
enden werde

(Berlin-Wilmersdorf, den 19. August 1975)

completely alone or *unio mystica* with the only pos-
sible partner end of consciousness thus everyone is a
partner and just right as a rotten meal for worms or
ashes ashes to ashes the amorphous form is life is
compromise temporarily until death that is absolute
I have just written down this poem in German that Minulescu
first published in nineteen hundred and thirteen
in Rumanian I quote it here and now I read it once more

(Neptune, August 12, 1975)

Epilogue in Berlin

Somehow I'm glad to be here again in the spaciousness of this city
with its dense traffic net in the mild light that doesn't press
down against the eyeballs when they are unprotected in the sun
that doesn't burn here full of emotion I took the S-Bahn I saw
the goldenrod bloom next to the railroad embankment about a
year ago Ludwig Harig gave this plant a great deal of attention
full of emotion and not without nostalgia I think of the Turks there
in the Bazaar Café Neptune who stirred until it was ready in the metal pot
with the little cups in the hot sand the coffee

Stirred with emotion by the rediscovery I saw the Grunewald pines
from the S-Bahn and I no longer thought they reminded me of the
pines in Upper Austria those of my youth of my childhood now they
reminded me of themselves and I thought I have really come to be
at home in this city at the Wannsee S-Bahn Station as I bought
shaving lotion I met Flavia suntanned she had been on Elba and
from my office I then sent poems of mine in German to blonde
Natasha who does not understand German far off at the Neptune
and I wrote in Rumanian to Vera in London

I sit at the dining room table in my own apartment drinking
red wine writing these lines next to me is the telephone
Angelica has just called me I interrupted this stanza and
don't think that I will end it

(Berlin-Wilmersdorf, August 19, 1975)

wir haben verloren

wir haben
die worte
verloren

die augen
die hände
den blick

aber
ich spüre
alles berührt uns

das licht
trifft jeden

und die erde
trägt uns

legende

wir sind
legende
totes bild

wir sind
ein leuchten
spät und mild

PETER PAUL WIPLINGER

(1939–)

Peter Paul Wiplinger was born in Haslach in 1939 and studied drama, literature, and philosophy at the University of Vienna. He published his first collection of poems, *Hoc est enim,* in 1966, and he has since seen his poetry translated into Serbo-Croatian and later into English (by Herbert Kuhner in *Borders/Grenzen* of 1977). This book was followed by *Gitter* [Bars] in 1980, and *Abschiede* [Departures] in 1981. Wiplinger is presently at work on a trilogy of fiction, the first part of which, in the form of a radio play, was broadcast in 1973.

Wiplinger is also a scholar, the editor of the papers of Max Reinhardt. He has won prizes and fellowships in both Vienna and New York. Wiplinger is a member of the Austrian P.E.N. Club.

we have lost

we have
lost
the words

our eyes
our hands
our sight

but
I feel
everything touches us

light
strikes everyone

and earth
bears us

legend

we are
legend
dead image

we are
a weak
and fading light

wir sind
nur abbild
einer welt
die mit uns selbst
zusammenfällt

wir sind verloren

eines zum andern

ein wort
zum andern
fügen

einen satz
an den andern
reihen

und am schluß
nichts verstehen

außer die welle
die sich an land
wirft

außer den wind
außer den schatten
außer die stille

tag und nacht

der pfauenschrei
am tag
und nachts
das flattern
dunkler wimpern
verhängt
ein leben voll
mit weißgestickten
sternen
und wege
die wir nie
gegangen sind

we are
only a reflection
of a world
that crumbles
with us

we are lost

one to another

to join
one word
to another

to place
one sentence
after another

and at the end
to understand nothing

beyond the wave
that strikes
the shore

beyond the wind
beyond the shade
beyond the silence

day and night

the peacock's cry
by day
and at night
the fluttering
of dark lashes
cover
a lifetime
embroidered
with white stars
and paths
we have
never traveled

ende

wir wachen
tag und nacht
die augen erblinden
sie sprengen
die wortbrücken
sie vernichten
das schweigen
sie verderben
den himmel
sie löschen uns aus

end

we stand watch
day and night
eyes go blind
they blow up
bridges of words
they destroy
silence
they ruin
the sky
they extinguish us

alptraum

unvermutet
in der arena
des freien wortes
ehe ich meinen stolz
decken konnte
sagtest du:
ein schwacher löwe
seit er die wildbahn
betreten hat
daran litt ich
geliebte

sterbestunde

ausgezehrt vom bösen geschwür
ist das gesicht so schmal so schwarz
sehr ähnlich dem seines vaters
jetzt ist die sterbestunde
sagte die fromme schwester
und in den plötzlich einsetzenden
schrei von wildgänsen hinein:
hör, die jäger kehren heim!
was sollten sie auch noch auf dem feld
da es schon dunkel ist
ja, was sollten sie noch dort
wenn ihrer einer hier im schmerz vergeht

GÜNTER UNGER

(1941 –   )

Born the son of a local politician in Eisenstadt, Günter Unger received his Ph.D. in modern Austrian history from the University of Vienna in 1967. He is employed by ORF in Burgenland as a director and cultural programmer, and he is a member of the Austrian P.E.N. Club.

Unger's poems have appeared in various journals and newspapers. His first collection, *Schreibfrüchte* [Fruits of writing] appeared in 1978.

nightmare

unexpectedly
in the arena
of free speech
before i could conceal
my pride
you said:
the lion is weak
now that he is
on the track of game
that depressed me
sweetheart

the hour of death

wasted away by a malicious tumor
his face is thin and black
resembling that of his father
this is the hour of death
said the pious sister
and suddenly
the wild geese shriek:
listen, the hunters are going home!
why should they stay in the fields
since it is now dark
yes, what should they do there
when one of them is dying here in pain

sinnesreiz

im erwachen blendet
ein goldenes auge
chiffre für den
tod vor der zeit?
oder ein launiger wink
mir zu weisen
daß hinter dem
was ist
du
immer gegenwart hast?

mattersburg / judengasse

über dachfirste
mondtrunkene platanenkronen
galoppieren chagalls pferde
sich paarend
mit sanften augen
und triefenden lefzen

turning on

when i awake
i am blinded
by a golden eye
the cipher
for early death?
or a capricious wink
to show me
that behind everything
you are always there?

mattersburg / judengasse

above the ridges of roofs
moon-soaked tops of plane trees
chagall's horses gallop
coupling
with soft eyes
and wet lips

Ohne Gedanken

tief in mir den Tod
dieses federleichte ungeborene Kind

so lebe ich fort
von Erzählung zu Erzählung

und mein Sprechen
ändert nichts
an meiner eingefleischten
Lautlosigeit

Dieses Messer

dieses Messer
hat mir schon lange in die Augen gestochen
ich habe lang gezögert
aber heute habe ich mir gedacht
jetzt in der Nacht oder nie
und heimlich habe ich deine Taschen durchsucht
und alle Laden

glaub mir
ich wollte es nicht stehlen um es zu besitzen
ich wollte es nicht stehlen
ich wollte mir nur diese Wunde zufügen
nur diesen einen Schnitt wollte ich
und nur mit diesem Messer wollte ich mich schneiden
dein Messer sollte es sein

damit ich
böse und listig

ERNST NOWAK

(1944 –)

Ernst Nowak published his first volume of poetry, *Entzifferung der Bildschrift* [Deciphering the script of images], in 1977. In addition to a collection of stories which appeared in 1974, Nowak has published two novels, *Der Unterkunft* [The shelter] in 1975 and *Das Versteck* [The hiding place] in 1978.

Without Thinking

death deep in me
this feather-light unborn child

that's how I live
from story to story

and my words
do not change
my deeply ingrained
silence

This Knife

this knife
has long stabbed my eyes
I have long delayed
but today I thought to myself
that it would be tonight or never
and I secretly went through your pockets
and all the drawers

believe me
I didn't want to steal it in order to own it
I didn't mean to steal it
I only wanted to use it to make this wound
I only wanted to make this one cut
and I only wanted to cut myself with this knife
wanted your knife to be the one

so that I
could say

sagen könnte
dieses Messer ist schuld
dieses Messer war es
deines
du bist schuld
nur damit du es weißt
es war dein Messer

angrily and cunningly
that this knife was to blame
it was this knife
yours
you're to blame
you should know
it was your knife

Dämmerung

Schleifmaschinen
zerren
im Morgengrauen
Gedanken
durch Mauerritzen
und Glasscherben.

In Kellern
hinter
vergitterten Fenstern
lagern
stapelweise
weiße Giftwürfel.

Auf dem
Balkongeländer
gehen
ahnungslos
die Tauben
spazieren.

Späte Tage

Späte Tage—kurze Tage,
Tage der Nebel,
Tage, die wie Trauerweiden
durch das Gitter der Zeit hängen,
löschen die Erinnerung

ILSE BREM

(1945 –   )

Ilse Brem was born in the Wachau, in Lower Austria, in 1945. She began her career as a writer quite recently. Since that time she has completed a radio play and has published poetry, prose, and essays in various journals. Her first collection of poems, *Spiegelungen* [Reflections], appeared in 1979. It was followed by *Beschwörungsformeln* [Formulas for Oaths] in 1982 and *Lichtpunkte* [Dots of light] in 1983. Ilse Brem is also a painter and a graphic artist; her work has appeared in several exhibitions throughout Austria.

Dawn

At dawn
grinding machines
drag
thoughts
through cracks in walls
and over broken glass.

In cellars
behind
barred windows
packages
of white poison
are piled up.

Up on the balcony railings
pigeons
walk around
aware
of
nothing.

Late Days

Late days—short days,
fog days,
days that hang through
the fence of time
like weeping willows
extinguish the memory

an frühe Tage,
jüngste Tage—lange Tage,
reißen sie in Stücke,
breiten den Schleier
des Vergessens darüber.
Späte Tage—kurze Tage,
Tage der Nebel,
Tage, die wie Trauerweiden
durch das Gitter der Zeit hängen,
beugen uns zur Erde,
zur Asche,
tilgen den Gedanken an das,
was wir waren
und wir sein wollten,
lassen uns selbst
in den Wind verstreuen,
nach Westen,
entgegen—der untergehenden Sonne.

Rosen

Diese Rosen anschauen,
einen Atemzug lang,
sie tausend Atemzüge lang
anschauen wollen
und nach dem hundertsten Atemzug
sich abwenden,
weil man auch Rosen nicht
tausend Atemzüge lang
anschauen kann.

Manchmal

Manchmal,
da seh' ich die Gräser
zu unseren Füßen zittern,
Gräser, deren Schärfe
du angenommen hast,
wenn du eine Sprache sprichst,
die ich nicht verstehen kann.
Dann schmerzt etwas in mir,
das das Atmen beschwerlich macht.
Es ist irgendwo
tief drinnen in mir.

of early days,
recent days—long days,
tear them to pieces,
spread the veil
of oblivion over them.
Late days—short days,
fog days,
days that hang through
the fence of time, like willows,
bend us to the ground,
to the ashes,
eradicate the thought
of what we were
and wanted to be
let us scatter ourselves
westward,
toward the setting sun.

Roses

Looking at these roses
for the duration of a breath,
wanting to look at them
for a thousand breaths
but turning from them
after the hundredth breath
since even roses
can't be looked at
for a thousand breaths.

Sometimes

Sometimes
I see grass
shivering at our feet,
grass whose sharpness
you have assumed
when you speak in a language
I cannot understand.
Then I feel a pain somewhere
that makes it hard to breathe.
It's somewhere deep in me.

Es ist nicht der Kopf,
nicht der Bauch,
nicht die Brust.
Es ist etwas viel Schlimmeres.
Ich weiß nicht, was es ist.

Not in my head,
nor my stomach,
nor my breast.
It's something much worse.
I don't know what it is.

———————

bei einem freund in der nervenklinik einer der besten
europas was wollen sie & wer sind sie zu ihm
die capos im weißen talar das zurück-ziehen der stimmen-schnippen der
      zigaretten-
stummel wenn sie vorbeipatrouillieren die knüttel
nicht sichtbar aber zu hören wer hier nicht spurt
kommt auf den schlimmeren pavillon sie stehen frühmorgens
an deinem bett & beobachten während der nacht
tagt die gerichtskommission man wird dich vielleicht
in ein insekt verwandeln ich würde euch alle
sagt einer der weißen vertilgen die ganze rasse du lachst
lauthals ein schwarzes lachen um dich herum
& hättest dich sagst du lachend schon informiert
über die ausbruchsmöglichkeiten aus gitterbetten

———————

was am anfang war
(der leviathan
oder sein ei)
hat man vergessen

gesprochen wurde
vermutlich
(wie sich's gehört)
der prolog
        es kann aber auch

PETER HENISCH

(1 9 4 3 –   )

Born in Vienna, Peter Henisch is a young writer of many talents. He has been at the center of the "Wasps' Nest Group" in his native city. He was awarded the Austrian State Scholarship for Literature in 1970. Henisch is presently the literary editor of *Neue Wege*.

A novelist and an essayist as well as a poet, Peter Henisch, in addition to his several collections of poems, has written a biography of his father, Walter Henisch (*Der kleine Figur meines Vaters* [The small image of my father] (1975), and a novel, *Der Mai ist vorbei* [May is over] (1978). Henisch is a member of the Graz Authors' Collective.

———

visiting a friend in one of the best asylums in
europe what do you want and what are you to him
the guards in white smocks the lowered voices the flicking of cigarette
butts when they pass on patrol with their clubs
hidden but audible one who is disobedient here
is taken to a worse ward early in the morning they stand
at the end of your bed & observe during the night
when the board meets to judge you perhaps
they'll turn you into an insect i would exterminate
all of you says one of the white ones the whole race you laugh
loudly black laughter all around you
& you have you say laughing already studied
the possibilities of making an escape from the barred beds

———

what was in the beginning
(the leviathan
or the egg)
has been forgotten

a prologue
in all likelihood
was spoken
(as is customary)
      but it is possible

(da noch gar nichts war
noch nicht einmal wände
um zuzuhören
ist das nicht sicher)
ein epilog
gewesen sein
und seither
(das ist eine arbeits-
hypothese)
    seither herrscht schweigen

alle dinge
sind durch dasselbe gemacht
und ohne dasselbe
ist nichts gemacht
was gemacht ist

in ihm war der tod
und der tod
ist das dunkel des menschen

und das dunkel
verdunkelt das licht

und das licht

    und das licht . . . (?)

————

aber das fleisch
ist wort geworden
(das wort
ist vom fleisch gefallen)

und trotz konträrer
behauptungen
zuständiger
ämter
hat auch das wort
keine bleibe gefunden
(ist immer
ein fremdwort geblieben)
in unseren engen
breiten

(since there was nothing at all
not even walls
to listen
everything is in doubt)
that it was
an epilogue
and since then
(this is a working
hypothesis)
    silence has reigned

all things
are made of the same
and without the same
nothing has been made
that is made

in it was death
and death
is man's darkness

and the darkness
darkens the light

and light

    and light . . . (?)

———————

but the flesh
has become word
(the word
has fallen from the flesh)

and in spite of
assurances
to the contrary
by qualified
authorities
the word too
has not found sanctuary
(has remained
a foreign word)
in our narrow
breadth

einer kam
für das licht zu zeugen

die für das dunkel zeugten
waren schon längst gekommen

einer kam
für das licht zu zeugen

für die finsternis zu zeugen
kommen unzählige

bitte
ich urteile sicher
nach quantitativen aspekten

aber daß sie die finsternis waren (sind)
behaupte ich nicht

sie waren nicht die finsternis
aber sie haben verfinstert

sie sind nicht die finsternis
aber im licht
stehen sie trotzdem

———

one came
to bear witness to light

those who bore witness to darkness
came a long time ago

one came
to bear witness to light

those who bear witness to darkness
are countless

pardon me
but i'm surely judging
by quantitative standards

but i don't claim
that they were (are) darkness

they were not darkness
but they have caused darkness

they are not darkness
but they certainly
obscure light

situation

mit verdrehtem hut
auf dem weißen stein
sitzt er ißt das brot
in der leichten luft
unter diesem wind
nimmt ein grünes blatt

hört

hört den weißen stein
tragend ihn der kaut
mit verdrehtem hut
mit dem brot dem blatt
unter diesem wind
in der leichten luft

pfeift

pfeift ein kleines lied
hält das blatt das brot
mit verdrehtem hut
auf dem weißen stein
in der leichten luft
unter diesem wind

sieht

sieht das lied in grün
und das blatt als brot
in der weißen luft
kaut den leichten stein
im verdrehtem wind
unter diesem hut

REINHARD PRIESSNITZ

(1 9 4 5 –   )

Born in Vienna after the war, Reinhard Priessnitz has achieved a reputation as an experimental poet. *vierundvierzig gedichte* [forty-four poems], Priessnitz's first collection, appeared in 1978. He is a founding member of the Graz Authors' Collective.

situation

with cocked hat
he sits on a white stone
eats a piece of bread
in the breezy air
under this wind
takes a green leaf

hears

hears the white stone
bearing the chewer
with cocked hat
with bread and leaf
under this wind
in the breezy air

whistles

whistles a little song
holding the leaf the bread
with cocked hat
on the white stone
in the breezy air
under this wind

sees

sees the song in green
and the leaf as bread
in the white air
chews the breezy stone
in the cocked wind
under this hat

landschaft

im rauchwald
der lippen wo
unsre pflanzen
spiralen spi-
ralen im

haarwald
des golds wo
nebel uns sonnt
und ich klebe
an deinem harz

im traumwald
mein tal wo
unser bett grünt
blatt bei blatt
und wir fallen hin-
unter zum

nachtwald
blut oder wunden
wimpernberauscht
und weiter und
lichten uns weiter
in wald und
in schlaf

fernschreiben

was weiß der amsel lied
rabenrot und rosenschwarz
was weiß der amsel lied
von meinem stein
von deinem leib?

was weiß der amsel leib
rosenrot und rabenschwarz
was weiß der amsel leib
von meinem lied
von deinem stein?

landscape

in smoke forest
of lips where
our plants
spiral spi-
ral in

hair forest
of gold where
fog suns us
and i stick
to your resin

in dream forest
my valley where
our bed turns green
leaf by leaf
and we fall
down to

night-forest
blood or wounds
rustling eyelashes
and farther and farther
lighting our way
into the forest
and into sleep

telegraph

what does the blackbird's song know
of raven-red and rose-black
what does the blackbird's song know
of my stone
of your body?

what does the blackbird's body know
of rose-red and raven-black
what does the blackbird's body know
of my song
of your stone?

was weiß der amsel stein
was weiß der amsel steinern herz
zu kupfer wird zur nacht der tau
von meiner schwarzen rose leib
von deines roten raben lied

what does the blackbird's stone know
what does the blackbird's stony heart know
of the dew of my black-rose body
of your crow-red song
which turn to copper at night?

notiz

ich pflege meinen garten
(ich habe keinen)
und
pflücke blumen
(die mir versprochen wurden)

ich züchte bienen
(in meinem garten)
und
verkaufe honig
(an längst verstorbene)

methode a

sich in gedichten
hinter wortbarrikaden
verstecken
weil man sprachlos ist

change

die ganze schraube
des schraubenraddampfers

HELMUT ZENKER

(1949 –   )

The youngest poet in the collection, Helmut Zenker was born in St. Valentin in Lower Austria in 1949. He has since established his reputation as a poet, novelist, and author of short stories, TV and radio scripts, and a children's novel. He began his career as a poet in 1968 and published his first collection, *Merkheft* [Notebook] in 1971. An experimental mixed-genre collection, *Aktion Sauberkeit* [Mopping up action], followed in 1972.

Zenker wrote two novels, *Kassbach* and *Kock,* in 1974 and 1975, respectively; a third, *Herr Novak macht Geschichten* [Mr. Novak makes history] was published in 1976, and *Das Froschfest* [The celebration of the frogs] appeared in 1977. Zenker's stories have also been collected, under the title of *Die Entfernung des Hausmeisters* [The removal of the janitor], in 1978. More recently Zenker has collaborated with film director Peter Patzak, notably in the prize-winning film version of Zenker's own novel, *Kassbach*. Zenker is a member of the Graz Authors' Collective.

note

i tend my garden
(I don't have one)
and
pick flowers
(that were promised to me)

i keep bees
(in my garden)
and sell the honey
(to those long dead)

method a

in poems
i hide behind
barricades made of words
because i'm speechless

change

the whole propeller
of the steamboat

ist tot
vögel nistern da
wo früher fische starben

fin

hier stand ein haus
hier stand dein haus
hier stand unser haus
hier war unsere stadt
hier war unser land
ruhet sanft!

is defunct
birds now nest
where fish once died

fin

a house stood here
your house stood here
our house stood here
this was our city
this was our country
rest in peace!

ACKNOWLEDGMENTS

We gratefully acknowledge the following permissions:

FRIEDRICH ACHLEITNER. From PROSA, KONSTELLATIONEN, MONTAGEN, DIALEKTGEDICHTE, STU-
DIEN, published by Rowohlt Verlag. Copyright © 1970 Rowohlt Verlag GmbH, Reinbek bei
Hamburg. Reprinted by permission of the author.

ILSE AICHINGER. From VERSCHENKTER RAT. © S. Fischer Verlag GmbH, Frankfurt am Main,
1978. Reprinted by permission of the publisher. "Belonging" was first published in *Austria
Today*, Vol. II, Autumn/Winter 1976. "Edge of the Mountain" is reprinted also by permission of
Logbridge-Rhodes, Inc. which controls the U.S. market for this poem.

H. C. ARTMANN. "A Rosn" from DIEWIENER GRUPPE, edited by Gerhard Rühm. Copyright © 1976
by Rowohlt Taschenbuch Verlag GmbH, Reinbek bei Hamburg. Reprinted by permission of
the publisher. Other poems from EIN LILIENWEISSER BRIEF AUS LINCOLNSHIRE. © Suhrkamp
Verlag, Frankfurt am Main, 1969. Reprinted by permission of Kurt Bernheim for Suhrkamp
Verlag. "Always birds" was first published in *Austria Today*, Vol. II, Autumn/Winter 1976.

INGEBORG BACHMANN. From INGEBORG BACHMANN—WERKE edited by Christine Koschel, Inge
von Weidenbaum, and Clemens Münster. Copyright © R. Piper & Co. Verlag, 1956, 1957,
1978. Reprinted by permission of Joan Daves for the publisher.

KONRAD BAYER. From DAS GESAMTWERK, published by Rowohlt Verlag. Reprinted by permission
of Traudl Bayer.

THOMAS BERNHARD. From AUF DER ERDE UND IN DER HÖLLE, published by Otto Müller Verlag,
Salzburg, 1957. Reprinted by permission of the author.

GERALD BISINGER. From POEMA EX PONTO, POETISCHE NACHRICHTEN AUS DER OSTLICHEN LA-
TINITAT, Erlangen, 1977. Reprinted by permission of the author.

WALTER BUCHEBNER. Poems copyright Walter Buchebner Gesellschaft.

ILSE BREM. From BESCHWÖRUNGSFORMELN, published by Edition Roetzer Gesellschaft m.b. H.
Reprinted by permission of the publisher and the author. "Late Days" appeared in *The New
Gazette*, No. 45, November 1980.

CHRISTINE BUSTA. From SALZGÄRTEN, published by Otto Müller Verlag, Salzburg and reprinted
with their permission. "Hoarfrost" appeared in *Dimension, Contemporary German Arts and
Letters*, Vol. II, No. 3, 1970. "Miserere," "They've cut down," and "An Angel in black" ap-
peared in *Poetry Australia*, No. 54, 1975.

PAUL CELAN. From DIE NIEMANDSROSE. © S. Fischer Verlag, Frankfurt am Main, 1963. Re-
printed by permission of the publisher.

ERICH FRIED. "Copyright" and "Vorteile einer Nacktkultur" from DIE BEINE DER GRÖSSEREN LÜ-
GEN; "Sprachlos" from DIE FREIHEIT DEN MUND AUFZUMACHEN; "Seifenblasen" from DIE
BUNTEN GETUME. All are reprinted by permission of Verlag Klaus Wagenbach, Berlin.
"Speechless" first appeared in *Mundus Artium*, Vol. XI, No. 2, 1979 and is reprinted by
permission.

GERHARD FRITSCH. From GESAMMELTE GEDICHTE, published by Otto Müller Verlag, Salzburg.
Reprinted by permission of the publisher and Barbara Fritsch. "August Moon" first appeared in
Poetry Australia, No. 69, 1979.

HERMANN GAIL. From EXIL OHNE JAHRESZEITEN, Vienna, 1972. Reprinted by permission of Bergland Verlag, Vienna. "Your sentence is written" and "I too could inject gasoline" appeared in INTERNATIONAL P.E.N. BOOKS ANTHOLOGY OF MODERN AUSTRIAN LITERATURE edited by Adolf Opel, published by Oswald Wolff (Publishers) Ltd., 1981. "I too could inject gasoline" and "A dwarf" appeared in *The International Portland Review,* 1980. Poems appear by permission also of David-Presse.

ALBERT PARIS GÜTERSLOH. From MUSIK ZU EINEM LEBENSLAUF, published by Bergland Verlag, Vienna, 1957 and reprinted with their permission. "August" first appeared in *Austria Today,* Vol. II, Autumn/Winter 1976 and in *Modern Poetry in Translation,* No. 29, Autumn 1976.

MICHAEL GUTTENBRUNNER. "Val d'Annivier," "Heimkehr," and "Der Abstieg" from GESANG DER SCHIFFE, published by Claasen Verlag, Düsseldorf, 1980 and reprinted with their permission. Other poems by permission of the author. "Val d'Annivier" appeared in *Poetry Australia,* No. 54, 1975, and "The Patient," "Homecoming," and "Hitler and the Generals" appeared in *Die Pestsäule,* October 1975.

PETER HANDKE. From THE INNERWORLD OF THE OUTERWORLD OF THE INNERWORLD by Peter Handke. Reprinted by permission of The Continuum Publishing Company. From DAS ENDE DES FLANIERENS, published by David-Presse and reprinted by permission. Excerpts from "An End to Idling" appeared in *Austria Today,* Vol. II, Autumn/Winter 1976.

PETER HENISCH. From WIENER FLEISCH UND BLUT, Vienna, 1975, published by Jugend und Volk Verlag. GmbH and reprinted with their permission. By permission also of the author. "What was in the beginning" and "one came" appeared in *Die Pestsäule,* October 1975.

ALOIS HERGOUTH. Poems published by Verlag Styria and used with their permission and permission of the author.

MARGARETHE HERZELE. From CARINTHIAN LOVE SONGS, Klagenfurt, 1979, published by Carinthia Verlag and used with their permission. "Mother Chaos" and "March Moon-Night" appeared in THE INTERNATIONAL PORTLAND REVIEW, 1980.

MAX HÖLZER. "Tische" and "Ein Flügelpaar" from MARE OCCIDENTIS, DAS VERBORGENE LICHT, CHRYSOPOS, Pfullingen, 1976. "Unberührbar" and "Opium" from DER DOPPELGÄNGER, GE-DICHTE, Pfullingen, 1959. Published by Verlag Günther Neske and reprinted with their permission.

ERNST JANDL. From JANDL FÜR ALLE. © 1974 by Hermann Luchterhand Verlag, Darmstadt und Neuwied and reprinted with their permission.

HEDWIG KATSCHER. From STEINZEIT, Vienna, 1977. Published by Bergland Verlag and reprinted with their permission. "Before Night" appeared in *Poetry Australia,* No. 54, 1975.

KURT KLINGER. From AUF DEM LIMES, Salzburg, 1980. Published by Otto Müller Verlag and reprinted with their permission. By permission also of the author. "Variations on Death" appeared in *The New Gazette,* No. 48, April 1981.

ALFRED KOLLERITSCH. From EINÜBUNG IN DAS VERMEIDBÄRE. © 1978 Residenz Verlag, Salzburg und Wien. Reprinted by permission of the publisher.

HERTHA KRÄFTNER. From DAS WERK, published by Edition Roetzer Gesellschaft m.b. H. and reprinted with their permission. "The Boy" and "Litany" appeared in *Die Wortmühle,* 1980.

OTTO LAABER. Reprinted by permission of Anna Laaber.

CHRISTINE LAVANT. From KUNST WIE MEINE IST NUR VERSTUMMELTES LEBEN edited by Armin Wigotschnig and Johann Strutz, Salzburg, 1978. Published by Otto Müller Verlag and reprinted with their permission.

JOSEF MAYER-LIMBERG. From FON DE MÖADA UND DE HAUSMASDA: GEDICHDA AUS ODDAGRING, Graz, 1973. Published by Verlag Styria. Reprinted by permission of the author.

FRIEDERIKE MAYRÖCKER. From AUSGEWÄHLTE GEDICHTE. © Suhrkamp Verlag Frankfurt am Main, 1979. Reprinted by permission of Kurt Bernheim for Suhrkamp Verlag.

CONNY HANNES MEYER. From DEN MUND VON SCHLEHEN BITTER, Salzburg, 1960. Published by Otto Müller Verlag and reprinted with their permission. In translation the poems also appeared in VOICES WITHIN THE ARK: THE MODERN JEWISH POETS edited by Howard Schwartz and Anthony Rudolf, Avon Books, 1980. Reprinted by permission of the publisher.

DORIS MÜHRINGER. "Als ich ein Kind war" and "Immer wieder" from GEDICHTE II, Vienna, 1969, published by Bergland Verlag. Reprinted by permission of the publisher. Other poems by permission of the author. "When I was a child" appeared in *Die Pestsäule,* October 1975.

ERNST NOWAK. By permission of the author. "Without Thinking" appeared in *Mundus Artium,* Vol. XI, No. 2, 1979.

WALTHER NOWOTNY. Reprinted by permission of the author. "I've divided" appeared in The International Portland Review, 1980, "The dreamdog" appeared in *Poetry Australia,* No. 58, 1976, and "The hands" appeared in *Skylark,* No. 45, 1982.

ANDREAS OKOPENKO. From GESAMMELTE LYRIK, Vienna, 1980. Published by Jugend und Volk and reprinted with their permission.

REINHARD PRIESSNITZ. Used by permission of the author.

GERHARD RÜHM. "Die nacht" and "gib mir die hand" from DIEWIENER GRUPPE edited by Gerhard Rühm. Copyright © 1976 by Rowohlt Taschenbuch Verlag GmbH, Reinbek bei Hamburg. Others from GESAMMELTE GEDICHTE UND VISUELLE TEXTE by Gerhard Rühm. Copyright © 1970 by Rowohlt Verlag GmbH, Reinbek bei Hamburg. Reprinted by permission.

ERNST SCHÖNWIESE. By permission of the poet. "Everything is only a reflection" appeared in *Austria Today,* Vol. II, Autumn/Winter 1976. "When someone dies" appeared in INTERNATIONAL P.E.N. BOOKS ANTHOLOGY OF MODERN AUSTRIAN LITERATURE edited by Adolf Opel, published by Oswald Wolff (Publishers) Ltd., 1981.

JUTTA SCHUTTING. From IN DER SPRACHE DER INSELN, Salzburg, 1973, published by Otto Müller Verlag. Reprinted by permission of the publisher. "Out there in the night there are houses" appeared in *Austria Today,* Vol. II, Autumn/Winter 1976. "Late afternoon doves" appeared in BROADSIDES AND PRATFALLS edited by Herbert Kuhner. Published by The Menard Press, 1976, and used with their permission. "It happened in the angel's shadow" and "give water to a thirsty dog" were published in *Modern Poetry in Translation,* No. 32, Winter 1977. Several translations were also published in *Poetry Australia,* No. 58, 1976.

THOMAS SESSLER. From DIE UNENDLICHKEIT WIRD BLEIBEN, Vienna, 1969. Published by Bergland Verlag and reprinted with their permission. "When the day," "In a tangled knot of humanity" and "The smoke" appeared in VOICES WITHIN THE ARK edited by Howard Schwartz and Anthony Rudolf, Avon Books, 1980. "I know" appeared in BROADSIDES AND PRATFALLS edited by Herbert Kuhner, published by Menard Press, 1976 and used by permission.

WILHELM SZABO. From SCHALLGRENZE, Vienna, 1974, published by Bergland Verlag and reprinted with their permission. "Haute Couture of Poetry" appeared in *Integratio,* 1972.

GÜNTER UNGER. From SCHREIBFRÜCHTE, Eisenstadt, 1978. Published by Edition Roetzer Gesellschaft, m.b.H. and reprinted with their permission. "Nightmare," and "turning on" appeared in *The New Gazette,* No. 47, March 1981.

PETER PAUL WIPLINGER. "Legend" and "end" appeared in *The Portland Review,* Vol. XXVII, No.

2, 1981. "We have lost" appeared in *Stardancer,* No. 56, Spring 1980. By permission of the poet.

HERBERT ZAND. From AUS ZERSCHOSSENEM SONNENGEFLECHT edited by Wolfgang Kraus, Vienna, 1973. Published by Europa Verlag and reprinted with their permission.

HELMUT ZENKER. "Change" and "method a" from AKTION SAUBERKEIT, Vienna, 1972. Published by Bergland Verlag and reprinted with their permission. Others by permission of the poet. "Note" appeared in *Mundus Artium,* Vol. XI, No. 2, 1979.

INDEX OF POETS

INDEX OF TITLES AND FIRST LINES
(GERMAN)

INDEX OF TITLES AND FIRST LINES (ENGLISH)